The
Sterilization
of
Carrie Buck

The
Sterilization
of
Carrie Buck

J. David Smith
K. Ray Nelson

NEW HORIZON PRESS
Far Hills, New Jersey

Library of Congress Catalog Card Number: 89-61444

J. David Smith
K. Ray Nelson
    The Sterilization of Carrie Buck

ISBN 0 88282 0451
New Horizon Press

For Joyce

and

To Carrie and Doris Buck and the thousands of others whose lives were forever changed because they were sterilized while at the State Colony for the Epileptics in Virginia. These individuals suffered a grievous wrong in the name of the rationalization which others described as "for their own good."

Contents

Acknowledgment

*T*he occasion of completing this book is a personal celebration for us. We have looked forward with great anticipation to sharing the story of Carrie Buck with interested readers. We relish seeing the manuscript that we have written, rewritten, and generally lived with for such a long time become a book. Our joy is magnified by having the opportunity here, on its beginning pages, to give words of thanks to those people who have been most supportive of our efforts to relate the facts and significance of the sexual sterilization of a young Virginia woman in 1927.

We were given invaluable assistance in our research for this book by several organizations and individuals:

Dr. Smith especially wishes to thank:

Commissioner Howard Cullum of the Virginia Department of Mental Health and Mental Retardation who granted me access to Carrie Buck's records at the Central Virginia Training Center. These records allowed me to understand and relate an important chapter of Carrie's life. I am in Commissioner Cullum's debt for recognizing the special circumstances of Carrie's case and the importance of her story's being told.

I am also enormously grateful to Senator Elliot Schewel of the Senate of Virginia for believing in the value of my work and who was an unfailing advocate in my quest to discover the details of Carrie's story.

Dr. Bill Walker, Director of the Central Virginia Training Center, greatly facilitated my work there and I appreciate the encouragement he gave me. Two of his staff members, Ms. Helen Hardy, Director of Medical Records, and Ms. Helen Hester, Professional Library Director, were also most gracious and helpful.

I was received with hospitality in the Manuscripts Division of Alderman Library at the University of Virginia. I am particularly appreciative of Michael Plunkett's help while I was reviewing the Aubrey Strode Collection there.

Martin Levitt was helpful and genuinely interested in my research during my several days at the American Philosophical Society.

The contact I had with people who had personal relationships with Carrie during her lifetime, or who knew her through family ties, brought a special quality to my understanding of her. I was given particularly valuable insights by Mr. and Mrs. A. T. Newberry, Mrs. Lucille Lewis, and Sharon Kincaid. By a delightful coincidence, my father-in-law, Fred Shaver, was able to send me to Jerry Layman, director of the nursing care facility where Carrie was a resident at the time of her death. Thanks to both.

From the start of my work on this book, I had the encouragement of my friend and colleague, Ed Polloway. He has been consistently tolerant of my obsessions and compulsions, and has often reassured me of the value of the work I have chosen to pursue. Rosel Schewel and Pete Warren have also been unfailing friends and have been mentors to me. I am lucky to have found them.

I was given assistance and support in this effort by the staff of the Lynchburg College Library. Such good people! The Committee on Faculty Research and Development at Lynchburg College provided some financial help for my research, and I am grateful. A major source of support was the Virginia Foundation for the Humanities. My freedom as a Fellow under the auspices of the Foundation allowed me to accomplish much of the research on the life of Aubrey Strode and my investigation of Carrie's family history.

My work on Carrie Buck's life was facilitated by those scholars who had previously investigated *Buck v. Bell* and related matters. I owe a great deal to the quality and care of their efforts. Primary regards in this respect are due Paul A. Lombardo.

Several people read early drafts of this book. Thanks go to Bob Lassiter, Ken West, Stephen Jay Gould, Mary Bishop and Tom Looney for helpful criticism and encouragement. I also appreciate the advice and interest of Hal Devening in the early stages of this work.

Phyllis Lane prepared the manuscript with care and good judgment. Through her fine work many of the mistakes in execution and expression were corrected. She is a trusted and respected colleague.

In addition to the above, Dr. Nelson gives special appreciation to:

Mrs. Juanita Cash, my secretary while I was Director of the Central Virginia Training Center, who received the inquiry that led to the location of Doris Buck, and eventually to Carrie Buck.

Mr. George Stoddard, a writer who went with me to visit Doris Buck Figgins, and whose newspaper article about that visit resulted in national attention being refocused on Carrie and Doris and the history of involuntary sterilization in America.

Finally, we are gratified with the confidence and trust invested in us and our telling of Carrie Buck's story by our publisher, Joan Dunphy and editor, Richard Gingrich. Without Joan's belief and support, *The Sterilization of Carrie Buck* might not be reaching its current audience. She has shown a concern for the importance of this book which is reflected in the quality of its presentation.

Foreword
by
J. David Smith

*I*n March of 1988, before Dr. Ray Nelson joined me as
co-author, I received a letter from Stephen Jay Gould.
His letter came as a reply to my having written to him
with the news that *The Sterilization of Carrie Buck* would
be published. I had shared with him earlier the first draft
of the manuscript, so it was with great excitement and
gratitude that I read the words of his letter.

Professor Gould's books, particularly *The Mismea-
sure of Man*, have been valuable sources of learning and
as vessels of encouragement. Stephen Gould shares his
scientific brilliance, his expressive talent and his sensi-

tivity to the human condition in ways that caution and inspire those who read his writings or listen to his lectures. He has not confined himself to university halls and academic publications. He has shared his expertise and insight with broader constituencies in a nation and world still struggling with old problems. Recently, for example, he served as an expert witness on evolution in a judicial revisit of the evolution/creationism curriculum issue by the Supreme Court. He has also personally taken his message of equality as a contingent fact of human history to southern Africa.

I was honored and elated to receive the words that follow from Stephen Jay Gould as an endorsement for the story of Carrie Buck. Both Dr. Nelson and I can not imagine a foreword for this book that would be more meaningful. We are pleased to be able to share it with you, the reader, as you begin this account of the intersecting of an individual human life with a social movement.

March 29, 1988

Dr. J. David Smith
Professor of Education and Human Development
Lynchburg College
Lynchburg, Virginia 24501

Dear Dave,

The story of Carrie Buck is the focal episode in a major story of 20th century social history. (I would compare it to the Scope's trial, which of course occurred at about the same time, as the key item in the history of a social and legislative movement not resolved until our Supreme Court victory of last year.) Eugenical sterilization surely had a greater impact on people's lives than creationism. Just think of the 40,000 sterilized in this country, not to mention the half million based on Germany's version of the law that Carrie Buck challenged and lost in the Supreme Court. Yet while books, not to mention television dramas, abound about the Scope's trial, no one has yet properly presented Carrie's story to a mass audience. I congratulate you on your effort.

Sincerely,
Stephen Jay Gould
Harvard University

Introduction

*D*uring October of 1927, Charles A. Lindbergh was in the final days of a sweep through all forty-eight states, completing a hero's tour for his solo, nonstop, transatlantic flight. On the 19th, a rainy Wednesday, Lindbergh's plane appeared out of a cloudy southwest sky and touched down at Logan Field in Baltimore, Maryland. Struggling from the plane, he was covered with a slicker to protect him in the open car and his triumphant parade through the downtown streets of the city began.

Ticker tape and drizzle mixed in the air as office workers craned their necks from windows to catch a glimpse of the "Lone Eagle," America's latest hero. *The News* in Lynchburg, Virginia reported that the crowds in Baltimore pressed so closely to the automobile in which Lindbergh was riding that police had difficulty keeping the way open.

October 19, 1927 was also a cloudy day in Lynchburg itself. At the State Colony for Epileptics and Feeble-minded, another historic event was occurring.

For this one, there would be no ticker tape and no parade.

There would be no celebration.

But the surgery performed that day at the hospital on the heights above Lynchburg would influence human history as surely as Lindbergh's flight across the Atlantic.

On that same early autumn day in 1927, a young woman named Carrie Buck was being sexually sterilized. Without her understanding of what was being done to her, or her agreement to allow the surgery, her capability to have children was taken away.

The operation to sterilize Carrie Buck came following the United States Supreme Court's decision earlier that year, upholding the right of Virginia to impose sterilization upon any person judged to be mentally defective.

Carrie Buck was the subject of the test case leading to that decision.

Fifty years later, when reporters questioned how she'd felt, Carrie would reply, "They just told me I had to have an operation, that was all."

1

Carrie's Childhood

---

*L*ater, when she spoke of her childhood, what Carrie remembered most vividly was "the endless work," "the servants' chores" and the feeling of "never being a family member in the house" in which she lived. The loneliness she had felt and seen followed her. She bore it stoically, but it showed in her dark, brooding eyes and permeated even the few happy moments of her life.

The small stone house on Grove Street in Charlottesville, Virginia, in which she lived for almost eighteen years, was really the house of J. T. Dobbs, his wife and daughter. Carrie had become the Dobbs' ward at age three, given into their care because it was said that her natural mother, Emma Buck, lived a desolate existence as a prostitute, bringing Carrie into a constant stream of seamy environments and relationships. Carrie had been Emma's first child, the only one born of Emma's marriage to Frank Buck. Some say Frank Buck died in an unfortunate accident, leaving his poverty-stricken widow to earn her living on the streets. Others insist he merely ran away from his own poverty stricken existence.

Though Carrie said of her years with the Dobbs, "I had good days and I had bad days," even as a small child she had been aware they were not her real parents. She referred to them only as "the Dobbs," never mother or father. The so-called adoption, of which they spoke afterward, was probably not a legal one, but an informal arrangement or "an act of kindness," as they so often put it.

And when, by chance, they met Carrie's natural mother in town, or heard some idle gossip from their neighbors about Emma's "loose ways," it was to this same "act of kindness" that they attributed the fact that Carrie too, despite her "bad blood," was not living on the streets as her mother and her younger half-sister Doris and half-brother Roy did.

It was in these few chance meetings that Carrie began to develop strong feelings for her mother. They were feelings of protectiveness, of caring that would endure over a lifetime—a lifetime in which they were often separated by the hardships and misfortunes that plagued both their lives—but which also served to forge a strong bond between mother and daughter, and even between Carrie and her half-sister Doris and her half-brother Roy, whom she was only to know in the few moments they crossed each other's paths on the streets of Charlottesville.

Perhaps the only really happy days of her childhood had been those she spent in school. Although it was later to be reported that she had been a dull child who had spent her time writing "notes to the boys in her class," the records of the McGuffey School in Charlottesville and the Midway School, the schools Carrie attended from 1913 to 1918, tell a much different story, one closer to Carrie's own memories of her school days.

School records indicate that Carrie was a very normal child. She attended classes for five years until the Dobbs withdrew her "to help with the chores at home." During that time, she progressed in proper sequence from grade to grade. Her last teacher recorded her assessment of Carrie as "very good—deportment and lessons"—and recommended her for promotion.

Through the years, she always remembered how much she had "liked going to school" even though she admitted, chuckling, that she had "played hooky too often." But life in the Dobbs' home consisted of much hard work and sometimes Carrie also did housework for other families in the neighborhood.

Taking a day off now and then to be with other classmates, or just to walk around town, seemed fun. Clean fun, for she "hadn't been into boys," she always insisted. "I didn't run around; I wasn't allowed to." Though the Dobbs "mostly treated me nicely" there was little frivolity, nor even the sense of encouraging normal boy-girl activities they accorded to their own daughter, who was about Carrie's age.

3

ILLUSTRATION 1: Charlottesville in the 1900's. Holsinger
Studio Collection, University of Virginia Library.

Carrie moved in a different plain; always suspect because of her mother's reputation, and always beholden because of her own inferior position in the household.

And, as she grew into a teenager, docile Carrie quietly accepted this status of caretaker for those about her as she would care for many others in her later years.

"Not that she hadn't liked boys," but for Carrie, shy, awkward and gangly, boys had been friends with whom to sneak down to the river and fish in her rare free hours or climb hills with—things other girls didn't like to do. She had not been wild like her half-sister Doris, who was always running off with this boy or that. Carrie "had not been into that sort of stuff." She was, as she herself put it, "a good girl."

So that when the Dobbs family insisted she had to get out of their home because she was pregnant, Carrie was bereft. According to Carrie, a member of their own family, their nephew, someone she had known and trusted, had raped her. She had told them the truth, but they preferred not to believe her and had begun to circulate stories that she was "having seizures" and was "morally delinquent." Carrie swore that none of it was true.

The nephew had raped her in the Dobbs' own home, acting as though Carrie had no rights except to submit to his will, and, because of it, she was to be turned out. The blame for the family's embarrassment caused by the pregnancy became Carrie's fault.

And they had found both a method and a route to rid themselves of her as quickly as possible. They would bring her case before the local court, having her certified as feeble-minded. It would be easy with her background and her relatives. And J. T. Dobbs knew exactly how the procedure worked. After all, he was a town peace officer, charged to deal with criminals and vagrants and the shiftless mentally retarded. He himself would file the necessary papers and deliver Carrie to the courthouse, just as he had delivered her mother three years previously on April 1, 1920.

2

Emma's Inquisition— April 1, 1920

---

*T*he dark-haired, swarthy-looking woman who stared around the court room was unkempt, overweight and shabbily dressed. But she had an unmistakable odor of sensuality about her that made the commission, assembled to decide whether to commit her to the Virginia Colony for the Epileptic and the Feebleminded, distinctly uneasy.

C. D. Shackelford, justice of the peace and judge for the proceedings, motioned for her to be seated.

But she did not immediately obey. Instead, she stood fidgeting, silently scanning the austere, high ceilings of

7

the room with its scarred benches and dark wooden floor. It was the first of April, but the musty cold room still felt like winter.

The examining physician, Dr. Davis, came forward to begin "the inquisition and interrogatories."

He cleared his throat and stared into her dark, defiant eyes. The woman stared right back.

"Be seated," Shackelford announced. Slowly she sat down in the chair provided.

Again the physician cleared his throat. "Name?" he began, his voice hesitant, uncertain.

"Emma Buck," she said, cocking her head to one side and running a sickly white-coated tongue, which he later declared hypertrophic, over her reddened lips.

"When were you born," he continued, his voice taking on a cutting edge.

She narrowed her eyes, "November 1872."

"And the day?"

She shrugged.

"You don't know the day?" he said exasperated.

Again she shrugged.

"Can you tell me where you were born?"

"Albemarle," she said, opening her mouth wide to form the vowel sound, almost as though it were the opening word of a familiar song. He noted the poor condition of her teeth.

"Where do you live now?" he asked.

"Charlottesville," again she drew out the syllables in that singsong manner.

Quickly, he jotted the information down and glanced up again, throwing her a furtive glance.

"Are you married, single or divorced," he asked with

a half-smirk. He had already been made aware, both by the Superintendent of the Colony, Dr. Priddy, and by the local gossip, of Emma's "mental peculiarity" which was manifested by "a lack of moral sense and responsibility."

"Widow," she murmured. He could barely suppress a knowing chuckle.

Next, he showed her some colors and common objects. He seemed surprised when she could distinguish them all. Indeed, she seemed to understand most of his words and the rudimentary commands he uttered, but, when he asked her to do a simple errand, she merely sat, as if dumbfounded, not moving.

"Could you give this book to the lady over there?" he asked again, slowly and succinctly. When she did not respond, he repeated his request twice.

The woman continued running her hands over her rumpled dress, but made no move to get up and obey. Whether she was being obstinate or simply did not understand, he couldn't be quite sure.

"I'm going to have to report that you can't do a simple errand," he said, petulantly looking at the other two physicians. She shrugged and continued to stare at him. He decided to try a different subject.

"Do you have children?"

She held up three fingers.

"Three?" he questioned.

She nodded her head.

"Any of the children been mentally defective?"

She shook her head, "No, there are not." Indeed, it was to be a prophetic statement.

Dutifully, he wrote "no."

They had reached the point in the interrogation

9

where he had to ascertain her physical condition. Grumbling, he began to examine her.

"Have you ever had any serious illness?"

She waited until he had begun to inspect her teeth, tonsils, ears and eyes. "Yes," she murmured, "pneumonia, rheumatism." She exhaled a fetid burst of air into his face as she sighed and added, "and syphilis."

He drew a deep breath and tried to repress a shudder of distaste. "Are you suffering from that affliction now?" he asked. She looked confused.

"Do you have syphilis now?" he asked again.

"You're the doctor," she said, matter-of-factly.

Disconcerted, he flipped through his sparse notes. "Yes, I see you do," he said, shaking his head and noting the confirmation of venereal disease.

"I'm going to test your sight and hearing now, Emma."

She nodded, and seemed to pay as little attention as possible during the tests. She asked no questions, volunteered no additional information, submitting to his requests almost disdainfully. Watching her, he thought, What had she to be disdainful of? Certainly not of him, a medical doctor, an official of the court, the decider of her future fate. Nevertheless, he hurried the perfunctory tests along so that they could be rid of her. He continued noting the aspects of her appearance which confirmed his preliminary diagnosis. "Distinctly untidy," he wrote and, where he was charged to record his "moral reaction," he wrote "notoriously untruthful." Though her answers seemed candid at present, these were the words used to describe Emma about town, words he and the others in the courtroom had often heard bandied about.

"Have you ever been convicted of a crime," he went on.

She stifled a yawn, "Yes. Prostitution."

He did not have to ask the next question. Gossip in town had already alerted him to the fact that she was guilty of "moral delinquency," even though she had never been confined to a reformatory, prison or place of detention for incorrigibility.

"And you were married?"

She nodded, "I told you I'm widowed."

"And you have illegitimate children?"

She nodded again, absentmindedly, not even looking at him.

Frowning, he wrote down, "Didn't conduct herself in a proper conjugal manner."

Her manner continued to irritate him, and he accelerated his questions, looking about the court room for support from his fellow physicians. They nodded sympathetically.

"And what occupation have you followed and with what success?" A tone of snobbishness crept into his voice.

"Occupation?" she looked confused.

This time he didn't waste a moment trying to explain. He wrote "no" with a flourish.

"You haven't supported yourself ever?" he went on quickly, as if expecting no answer.

For the first time, Emma objected vehemently. "I have some income from my father's estate," she said with dignity, "My father was Richard Harlow. He was a man of property." Her voice took on an unmistakable ring of pride, "He died of spinal trouble. Mother died in childbirth."

Dr. Davis looked at her with disdain. "You could do housework, I suppose," he paused, "under supervision."

Flashing him an angry look, she turned away and fixed her attention on some non-existent spot on the ceiling. She made no further effort to answer.

As quickly as possible, he concluded the cursory mental examination. There wasn't much more to record beyond the fact that she could count to ten and that, as far as he knew, she had never been given any approved mental testing. The examination ended and, as speedily as possible on that first day of April 1920, Justice of the Peace C. D. Shackelford signed Emma Buck's Order of Commitment to State Colony for Epileptics and Feeble-minded Commonwealth of Virginia (City) of Charlottesville, to wit:

> To the Sheriff, or Sergeant, of the county or city of *Charlottesville* and to *Dr. A. S. Priddy* MD Superintendent of the State Colony for Epileptics and Feeble-Minded of *Madison Heights* Greetings:
> Whereas, I *C. D. Shackelford*, A Justice, or judge of said county of Charlottesville and *J. G. Flippen* and *W. H. Turner Jr.*, two physicians, the said *J. S. Davis* being the physician to the said *Emma Buck*, constituting a commission of inquiry, etc., into the mental condition of the said *Emma Buck*, has this day adjudged the said *Emma Buck* to be *Feeble-Minded*, and a suitable subject for an institution, for the care and treatment of the *Feeble-Minded*, and a citizen of this State, and without means of support and no person

appearing before me to give bond with sufficient security to be approved by me, payable to the Commonwealth with condition to restrain and take proper care of the said *Emma Buck* person, without cost to the Commonwealth, until the cause of confinement shall cease for the said *Feeble-Minded*, I, *C. D. Shackelford*, do in the name of the Commonwealth, Command you, the said sheriff, or sergeant, to make provisions for the suitable and proper care and custody of the said *Feeble-Minded* person and you the said Superintendent of the Colony for Epileptics and Feeble-Minded, are hereby required to receive into the said Colony, and into your care and charge, if there be a vacancy, in the said Colony, the said *Emma Buck* to be treated and cared for as a *feeble-minded* person; and I do herewith transmit to you, the said superintendent of the Colony for the Epileptics and Feeble-Minded, the interrogatories and answers thereto, taken by said Commission, touching the mental condition of the said *Emma Buck* and also the adjudication of the mental condition of the said *Emma Buck*, a copy of each of which has this day been delivered by me to the clerk of the court of the said city.

The Order of Commitment was supported by the three physicians: J. S. Davis, the mental examiner, J. C. Flippen, M.D. and W. H. Turner, M.D.

I, *J. S. Davis*, citizen of Virginia, physician and practitioner in the county of Albemarle, hereby certify that I have examined *Emma Buck* and find that

13

she is feeble-minded, within the meaning of the law, and is a suitable subject for an institution for *feeble-minded*, the patient's bodily health is *poor* and *she* has no contagious disorder.

The Order was further substantiated by the findings and adjudication of the Commission of the Commonwealth of Virginia, County of Albemarle.

Whereas, Emma Buck, who is suspected of being feeble-minded or epileptic . . . , was this day brought before us, *C. D. Shackelford*, Judge or Justice of said County and *J. C. Flippen* and *W. H. Turner, Jr.*, two physicians (said *J. S. Davis* being the physician of said suspected person) constituting a commission to inquire whether the said *Emma Buck* be feeble-minded . . . and a suitable subject for an institution for the care, training, and treatment of feeble minded or epileptic persons: and whereas the judge or justice has read the warrant and fully explained the nature of the proceedings to the said suspected person, and we the said physicians have in the presence (as far as practicable) of the said judge, or justice, by personal examination of witness, satisfied ourselves as to the mental condition of the said *Emma Buck*, we, the said judge or justice, and physicians constituting the commission aforesaid, de decide this day that the said *Emma Buck* is feeble-minded, and ought to be confined in an institution for the feeble-minded.

Five days later, on April 6, 1920 at 8:30 p.m., Emma Buck was admitted to Ward V of the State Colony for the Epileptic and Feebleminded. According to the Charge Attendant, A. Jones, she brought with her, "$4.80, waist shirt, overshoes, 1 pr. shoes, 1 pr. hose, 1 coat, hat, undershirt 2, skirt."

The clothes, the attendant noted, were "in very bad condition."

Emma always insisted that she had not been indigent as the court said and her lack of possessions would seem to indicate. She insisted that her family had left her some money. In view of later findings about her family, she may well have been correct. However, only a few half-hearted inquiries were made in her behalf, such as Dr. Bell's letter three years later to Caroline Wilhelm, a social worker in Charlottesville.

April 3, 1923

Miss Caroline E. Wilhelm
Charlottesville, Virginia

My Dear Miss Wilhelm:

Carrie Buck's mother, Emma Buck, who was committed to this institution five years ago from Charlottesville, claims that she has about $460.00 on deposit in one of the banks of Charlottesville, which came to her through the sale of some land that the family had owned. I am going to impose on your time and willingness to the extent of using you to get in touch with the various banks in Charlottesville and ask if such a person had an account there, or has money on deposit.

Emma claims that the money was deposited in the "New National Bank" but she does not know the name. I wish to thank you in advance for this favor and express the hope that you get up this way to see us sometime.

Very truly,
J. H. Bell, M.D.
Superintendent

These inquiries had little effect. Emma Buck was to remain institutionalized for the rest of her life. Twenty-four years later, she died of pneumonia. The note on her chart read "disposition of body: buried in Colony Cemetery grave 575 on April 19, 1944."

Eight days after her death, her son and daughter came to the Colony to inquire about their mother. "They did not know until their arrival to the hospital that she was dead," officials said. Though upset, "they were most considerate and accepted the explanation that authorities had been unable to reach Emma's other daughter, Carrie Buck."

3

Carrie's Commitment

---

*I*n the fall of 1923, J. T. Dobbs and his wife, Alice, petitioned the Honorable Charles D. Shackleford, Justice of the Peace and Judge of the Juvenile and Domestic Relations Court for the City of Charlottesville, Virginia— the same court official who, three years previously, had committed Carrie's natural mother, Emma Buck—to commit their foster child, Carrie Buck, to the State Colony for the Epileptic and Feebleminded.

According to their testimony, Carrie, since the age of eleven, had exhibited symptoms of feeble-mindedness and epilepsy. Currently, they stated, these symptoms had worsened, making it impossible for them to control or care for her any longer. Though they had provided for her "as an act of kindness," Mr. Dobbs' monthly wages were no longer financially adequate to continue to do so.

Judge Shackleford appointed a Charlottesville physician, Dr. J. F. Williams, and the Dobbs' family physician, Dr. J. C. Coulter, to examine Carrie, after which time he would institute a hearing at which the Dobbs family and Carrie herself would be required to testify as to the details of Carrie's alleged illness.

The reports of the two doctors agreed that Carrie Buck was, in their judgments, "feeble-minded within the meaning of the law."

When Carrie's foster parents were questioned before the hearing, they added to the picture being painted of Carrie as a strange, ungovernable girl, subject to "hallucinations and outbreaks of temper" and born with a mental condition characterized by certain "peculiar actions." Furthermore, they testified, she was dishonest and morally delinquent.

According to the Dobbs, Carrie had been born in Albemarle County and, at the time of her birth, her parents, Emma and Frank Buck, were unmarried. Later, they told the court, her mother had been diagnosed as feeble-minded and was now an inmate of the same institution in which the Dobbs desired to place Carrie. Her father's whereabouts were unknown.

The Dobbs said they had received Carrie at the age of three from her mother, whom they referred to as Mrs. Emmett (sometimes called Emma Buck). Carrie had lived with them at their Grove Street house since then, attending school up to the sixth grade. She was, they stated, able to read, write, recognize and distinguish objects, but not to take "proper notice of things."

Although the Dobbs family were quite certain that Carrie was feeble-minded, they were equally certain that she was capable of protecting herself against ordinary dangers without an attendant. They were equally uncertain about when her epileptic symptoms had appeared, saying at one point that her epilepsy had first appeared in childhood and, later, that they could not actually remember her being "subject to epilepsy, headaches, nervousness, fits or convulsions."

Carrie had little to say at the hearing, assuming that whatever was about to be done for her would be in her best interests.

The hearing was held on January 23, 1924. At its conclusion, Judge Shackleford ruled, as he had in her mother's case, that the doctors' opinions of Carrie Buck were correct. His judgment was that Carrie Buck was a suitable subject for an institution for the care and treatment of the feeble-minded. He ordered her delivered to the Superintendent of the Colony for Epileptics and Feebleminded at Lynchburg, Virginia without further delay.

But a delay was unavoidable.

Seventeen . . . and unmarried . . . Carrie Buck was pregnant.

In March of 1924, a month before Carrie's baby was due, Miss Caroline Wilhelm, the social worker to whom Dr. Bell had written abut Emma Buck, wrote to Dr. A. S.

Priddy, the superintendent of the State Colony, concerning Carrie's commitment papers. Miss Wilhelm was writing on behalf of the Red Cross in Charlottesville. In the letter, she mentions that the papers had been returned and were in the hands of attorney Homer Richey, who served on the Board of Public Welfare in Charlottesville and often attended to legal matters for the board:

> My dear Dr. Priddy:
>
> We are very sorry that the papers in this case have been so delayed. We did not know until a few days ago that they had been returned . . . for corrections and were still in the office of Mr. Richey who had agreed to make the necessary changes.
>
> We are writing now to urge that the case be acted upon as soon as possible. Mrs. Dobbs, in whose care the girl has been, is expecting to be called away almost any day to care for her daughter during her confinement [late pregnancy and delivery] and she does not wish to leave the girl alone.
>
> As Carrie Buck is expecting her baby about the middle of April, it is very important that she be admitted to the Colony before that time if it can be arranged.
>
> > Very truly yours,
> > [Miss] Caroline E. Wilhelm
> > Secretary

In response to her letter, as well as one from attorney Richey, urging that the commitment be expedited and arguing that all the papers were in order, on March

13th, Dr. Priddy insisted that the letter of the law be followed:

> . . . am satisfied that due process of law has not been observed in this case.
>
> I refer you to Sect. 1978 of the Code 1920, page 376 'Petition to have person declared feeble-minded.' This section recites that no feeble-minded person shall be sent to any institution except as hereinto-fore . . . provided. It provides that a petition shall be regularly filed, which was done in her case, and in the following Section 1079 it says thereupon it shall be the duty of the Judge or Justice with whom such petition is filed, to execute a warrant ordering such alleged feeble-minded person to be brought before him and to summon her custodian, etc. The Court of Appeals of Virginia has in more than one case declared any commitment illegal in which there was no warrant issued and it furthermore requires the warrant to be read to the person suspected of being feeble-minded or insane and that he is acquainted with the charge. One of the cases to which I refer was that of Mallory vs. Va. State Colony for Feeble-minded . . . , so I must have a warrant properly executed or I cannot accept the ward as legal.

> Very truly,
> A. S. Priddy
> Superintendent

The next day, Priddy wrote to Caroline Wilhelm and advised her that, even with her papers in order, Carrie

Buck could not be committed until after she had delivered her baby.

> My dear Miss Wilhelm,
>
> I have your letter of 11th inst. relative to the admission of Carrie E. Buck and note that you say she is expecting her baby about the middle of April and it is very important that she be admitted to the Colony before that time. I am sorry but we make it a rule to positively refuse admission of any expectant mothers to the Colony. You will have to make some provision to keep her until the child is born and disposed of and then on notification we will take her when the law has been complied with in committing her. I have advised Mr. Richey that he will have to send me a copy of the warrant on which she was committed. Very truly,
>
> A. S. Priddy
> Superintendent

Dr. Priddy was quite aware of the importance of complying with the full letter of the law. He had already been involved in *Mallory v. Priddy*, a case in which he was found not guilty (March 1, 1918) of intentionally sterilizing an illegitimate young girl during a normal abdominal operation. In a later appeal, *Mallory v. Virginia Colony for the Feebleminded* (June 13, 1918), he was again acquitted of the charges, but the court concluded that certain practices were not quite within the confines of the 1916 law concerning feeblemindedness.

Although conscious of legal parameters, Dr. Priddy,

nevertheless, considered his power as a physician absolute. At Carrie's subsequent trial, he would aver, "I have a right to do whatever is best for the physical and mental advantage of the patient."

On May 5th, a letter came to Dr. Priddy from Miss Wilhelm, explaining that Carrie's baby had been born and she was now ready to enter the Colony. She also described the arrangements which had been made for the baby.

My dear Dr. Priddy,

It has been very difficult for us to decide what disposition to make in the case of Carrie Buck as we feel that a baby whose mother and grandmother are both feeble-minded ought not be placed out in a home for adoption. However, the people who have had Carrie in their home ever since she was a little girl, are willing to keep the baby with the understanding that it will be committed later on if it is found to be feeble-minded also. We are therefore anxious to send Carrie to you as soon as possible and should be glad to know when you can receive her.

Can you send someone for Carrie, or send us transportation for an attendant for her.

Very truly yours,
(Miss) Caroline Wilhelm
Secretary

Dr. Priddy responded to Miss Wilhelm on May 7th with a letter which opened the way for Carrie's commitment to the Colony. This letter would alter the course of Carrie's life, and her experience would effect the lives of thousands of other people.

Dear Miss Wilhelm:

Replying to your letter of the 5th about Carrie Buck will say that I cannot advise you what disposition to make of the baby other than to place it in the City Almshouse. Of course, should this child be ascertained to be feeble-minded we will receive it here. However, the law puts a limit of 8 years in feeble-minded cases and we could not take it until it is eight years of age. I am enclosing transportation for attendant and her (Carrie) to Lynchburg. If you will kindly fill in name of attendant and advise me on what train she will arrive we will meet her at the station. The early morning local train comes into the Union Station at 9 A.M. and is the most convenient one for us to meet and whoever comes with her could return on the 12 o'clock train.

Very truly,
A. S. Priddy
Superintendent

Boarding the early train, Carrie and Carolyn Wilhelm made their way to the hospital in Madison Heights, overlooking the James River, Lynchburg and the mountains.

The 1905 will of S. R. Murkland of Amherst County had left a parcel of land to Western State Hospital. It consisted of about two hundred acres on the James River looking down from the heights north of Lynchburg. The purpose of this gift was to provide "extra comforts" for the patients of that hospital. Mr. Murkland's epileptic son was being cared for in that institution, which was nearly eighty miles away from the farm willed to it.

In February of 1906 the Virginia State Legislature passed an act authorizing the Board of Directors of Western State Hospital and the General Board of State Hospitals to build on the Murkland tract a facility for the care, treatment and employment of three hundred epileptic patients. Through Mr. Murkland's generosity and compassion, the Virginia State Epileptic Colony was to become an institution of the State of Virginia.

This action, however, did not come easily. The legislature had not yet acted on the matter in 1906 when Senator Aubrey Strode of Amherst explained, in a letter to a physician friend, Dr. George Harris, that the bill was meeting with some resistance. Apparently the economic benefits of the placement of the institution had become a matter of considerable political interest:

Dear Doctor:

We have only a fair chance of getting our Epileptic Colony Bill through. The House Committee on Prisons and Asylums gave the bill a unanimously favorable report and it is now on the calendar in the House. In the Senate committee, however, we have as yet been unable to take up the bill because of the press of other matters, but hope it will reach it next week.

We will need all the help we can get, as such institutions are much sought after and even if we succeed in having it established, some other locality may endeavor to offer inducements to switch it away from the Murkland farm, but we will do the best we can in the matter. It would not be a bad idea if you could get any of your friends in Lynchburg interested in the matter . . .

The Board of State Hospitals was also slow in moving the matter along. Again Strode intervened. In February of 1907 he wrote about the situation to L. W. Lane, the Commissioner of Hospitals:

Dear Sir:

Please kindly advise me of the latest action taken by the Hospital Board in reference to the Epileptic Colony which it was directed to establish on the Murkland land in Amherst County by the act approved February 20, 1906, and for which $25,000.00 was appropriated, one-half thereof being available before March 1, 1907.

Any information that you can give me in reference to the steps taken by your board up to this time to comply with this act will be appreciated.

Yours respectfully,
A. E. Strode

Throughout the establishment process, Strode, who was later to be the prosecuting attorney in the case of *Buck v. Bell*, exerted his personal energy and political influence. Contained in his collected papers are copies of letters he constantly wrote to other politicians, hospital superintendents and State Hospital Board members on matters related to the establishment of the institution. He was clearly an important force, indicated by the fact that when the Governor finally appointed the three members of the Board of Directors to manage the affairs of the new Colony for Epileptics, Irving P. Whitehead was one of the prominent members.

Irving P. Whitehead had been a childhood friend of Aubrey Strode. They had grown up on adjoining Amherst farms and remained friends and professional associates throughout their lives. Ironically, but not completely by accident, Irving Whitehead was later to be the attorney appointed to defend Carrie Buck's interests in her sterilization test case.

The Board of Directors assumed their offices in April of 1910. That same month, they selected Dr. Albert Sidney Priddy to be the first superintendent of the Virginia State Colony for Epileptics.

Albert Priddy was born of an old and respected Virginia family in 1865. His genealogy traced back to an ancestor who had come to the Colonies in 1650.

Dr. Priddy received his academic preparation in a private school then known as Shotwell Institute. He later studied medicine at the College of Physicians and Surgeons in Baltimore. He practiced medicine in Keysville, Virginia, his hometown, until 1901. It was then that he took a position as assistant physician at Southwestern State Hospital. In 1906 he was appointed superintendent of that institution.

Priddy had always taken an active interest in politics, successfully merging his two professions. He represented Charlotte County in the Virginia House of Delegates from 1893 until 1894 and again from 1900 to 1901. During his service in the General Assembly he was a member of the committee on prisons and asylums, and was one of the authors of a law providing pensions for Confederate veterans who had become disabled since the war. In 1900 he was patron in the House of a successful bill which addressed issues relating to the governance of state hospitals and the care of the "insane." In 1901 he was a member of the joint committee which adopted plans for the improvement and rebuilding of the Virginia Penitentiary.

The choice of Albert Priddy as the Colony's first superintendent was understandable in light of his past experience as superintendent of Southwestern State Hospital and his political involvement with matters concerning state institutions. He had political connections with Aubrey Strode, since both were Democrats and from the same region of the state. He also had both a political and professional relationship with Dr. J. S. DeJarnette, the superintendent of Western State Hospital. DeJarnette was a power and influence broker within the system of state institutions, and a true believer in eugenics.

Politically and philosophically, Albert Priddy was the perfect choice.

Almost immediately after assuming the superintendency, Priddy cemented his DeJarnette connections by making clear in the institution's public record that he subscribed to the eugenic philosophy advocated by DeJarnette and others in the state hospital bureaucracy at that time. In his first annual report written in 1910, he made it very clear that he believed epilepsy to be a genetic problem:

> . . . The epileptic remains with us always, alike the poor, as one of the most pitiful, helpless and troublesome of human beings, with their various and numerous afflictions, and worst to contemplate is the fact that of the known causes which contribute to the development and growth of epilepsy, that of bad heredity is the most potent, and with the unrestricted marriage and intermarriage of the insane, mentally defective and epileptic, its increase is but natural and is thus to be reasonably accounted for.

Dr. Priddy's second annual report in 1911 included an invocation that he was to repeat over and over for a decade. He issued a challenge to the state's lawmakers that was to finally reach fruition in 1924.

> It is reasonable to anticipate a rapid increase in epileptics and mental defectives. Therefore, it seems not inopportune to call the attention of our lawmakers to the consideration of legalized eugenics.

Thus a public call for compulsory sterilization had been issued.

From the time it was established, the Colony had admitted some people who were mentally retarded as well as epileptic. During its early years, increasing numbers of people who were mentally retarded but not epileptic were admitted. Finally, by 1914, the mission of the

Colony had been officially expanded to include people classified as feeble-minded. Soon, Priddy was focusing his eugenic concerns on that group and emphasizing connections between feeblemindedness, crime, alcoholism, prostitution and other social problems. In his 1915 report from the Colony he spoke of feeblemindedness in forewarning terms:

> This blight on mankind is increasing at a rapid rate . . . unless some radical measures are adopted to curb the influences which tend to promote its growth, it will be only a matter of time before the resulting pauperism and criminality will be a burden too heavy . . . to bear.

Priddy's statements in his annual reports concerning the "menace" of hereditary feeblemindedness and the socially therapeutic effects of sterilization increased in length and intensity. This escalation seems to have reached its peak in his 1922–23 biennial report. This would be the last report he would write prior to the successful passage of the Sterilization Act and the initiation of the Carrie Buck test case. In this report, Priddy targeted the "high grade defective" or "moron" as a major source of social problems and as the most appropriate candidate for sterilization.

A few years earlier, Henry Goddard had coined the term "moron" from a Greek word meaning foolish. The label soon came to be applied widely to people who were considered "high grades"—those who were not retarded seriously enough to be obvious to the casual observer and who had not been brain damaged by disease or injury. Morons were characterized as being intellectually dull, socially inadequate, and morally deficient. Priddy wrote:

High Grade Morons of the Anti-Social Class

Each day (working) in the custodial care of delinquent high-grade moron girls and women of good physical strength and health impresses me with the gravity of the responsibility which the . . . management of institutions for the feeble-minded assume in keeping these people . . . indefinitely to enforce morality in act or rather to restrain them from overt acts of immorality. If they are to be kept from indulging in sexual immorality it means they are to be kept a lifetime in institutions under the strictest custody . . . This to any fair-minded thinker must appear to be a cruel and unjust degree of punishment for their weaknesses . . . Besides the humane aspect of it a large percent of the girls and women of this class should be earning their own living in work for which they are mentally and physically adequate, rather than to constitute lifetime burdens on the taxpayers of the State. If they are to be kept in institutions and supported at the expense of the State for the child-bearing period covering at least thirty years, to prevent them from bearing children to increase the population of mental and physical defectives and dependents . . . it certainly seems more humane and just to them to give them the benefit of a milder and less severe method of attaining the desired end . . . Therefore, every reasonable and fair-minded person must concede that the withdrawal of the right to propagate their kind could and should be given to society in such cases of females as have demonstrated their constitutional mental and moral inability to use the right of child-bearing as a blessing to humanity rather than a curse.

Priddy goes on to state that many women were being classified as feeble-minded primarily on the basis of their sexual behavior rather than evidence of impaired mental function. In Priddy's eyes at least, "moral deficiency" had become synonymous with "mental deficiency."

. . . the admission of female morons to this institution has consisted for the most part of those who would formerly have found their way into the red-light district and become dangerous to society . . . If the present tendency to place and keep under custodial care in State institutions all females who have become incorrigibly immoral it will soon become a burden much greater than the State can carry. These women are never reformed in heart and mind because they are defectives from the standpoint of intellect and moral conception and should always have the supervision by officers of the law and properly appointed custodians.

Priddy continued his comments with a discussion of sterilization. He revealed that sterilization had evidently already become a practice at the Colony, at least in his operating room.

No one could be more opposed to a drastic and far-reaching law providing for the sterilization of mental defectives without careful safe-guard . . . (however) I view it as the only solution of the problem of the custodial care of them by the State . . . Within the last seven years between seventy-five and a hundred young women patients in this institution have had operations for pelvic diseases which rendered them sterile, and, after long observation, discipline and training, the most of them have been paroled in good families and have earned their living and led happy and useful lives, and I cannot recall that a single one has ever returned to the institution or against whom complaint has been made by officers of the law as to immorality. Many of them have married hard-working men of a slightly higher mental grade and have conducted themselves properly as married women. The paroling of unsterilized, physically attractive young women from the institution (to the) best of families is not without danger . . . it is not infrequent for them to be returned to the institution pregnant despite the best of care which was given them. The operation (sterilization), when carefully performed by a skillful operator, is as free from danger to life as any minor surgical operation can be, and it in no way effects the general health and normal functioning of any woman . . .

The superintendents of the four State hospitals and the Colony have been appointed a committee by the General State Hospital Board to draft a bill to be presented in the coming General Assembly for a law authorizing the sterilization of such patients as may be found capable of earning their own living and of being released under proper custodial care, without danger to themselves and the public. It is to be hoped that with the best legal talent to draft such a bill, it can come within constitutional limits and enacted into a law.

The fact that Albert Priddy had diagnosed so many cases of pelvic disease, and that the surgery he performed in these cases so often rendered his patients sterile, is difficult to accept as a coincidence. It seems evident that the medical diagnosis of pelvic disorder allowed Priddy to intervene in the reproductive potentials of these women. He was able to do, in the name of disease, what he could not as yet legally do in the name of eugenics.

Priddy had included similar statements concerning pelvic diseases and sterilization in previous reports. His didactic account in 1923, however, is even more remarkable in light of the fact that one of his earlier "therapeutic" sterilizations had resulted in *Mallory v. Priddy*.

In November of 1917, A. S. Priddy received a letter concerning one of the residents of his institution. Although the mechanics and grammar of the writing lacked precision and polish, the message and intent was quite direct and forceful. The writer of the letter, George Mallory of Richmond, accused Albert Priddy of breaking up his family. In his rough and imperfect, but forceful, language, Mallory threatened to cause trouble for Priddy unless his daughter was returned to him unharmed. He argued that his daughter was not feeble-minded and had no need to be in Priddy's institution. He also pointed out that he knew there was no legal basis for sterilization ("no law for such treatment") in Virginia. Mallory was fearful that his daughter would be sexually sterilized if she remained under Priddy's control much longer.

Mallory's anxiety had a very real foundation; Dr. Priddy had already sterilized George Mallory's wife and another one of his daughters. His letter to Priddy crackled with anger and desperation.

Priddy's response was instant and vehement. Accusing Mallory of threatening him, he informed him that if he dared to write another letter of that kind, he would have him arrested and committed to the Lynchburg institution. Priddy claimed that he had performed surgery on Mallory's wife and daughter at their request and because it was indicated as treatment for diseases they had. He closed his note by repeating that if he received further threats from Mallory he would have him "arrested in a few hours."

Mallory, however, may not have been a man of grammar, but he was not a man to be taken lightly. He sued. Priddy's own letter was presented as evidence against him to the jury in the case of *Mallory v. Priddy*. The case helped to illustrate clearly the kinds of social policies and practices that contributed to the passage of Virginia's involuntary sterilization law. It was also indicative of the kinds of "pelvic diseases" that Priddy encountered so frequently at the Colony, most of which seemed to have resulted in sterilization.

Paul Lombardo's scholarly examination of the case of *Mallory v. Priddy* includes the following facts which help to explain the exchange of letters between the two men and the subsequent court case.

On a balmy September evening in 1916, George

Mallory was away from his Richmond home working in a sawmill. While two family friends were visiting in the Mallory house, police officers entered and charged Mrs. Mallory with running a brothel. They arrested her, her nine children and the two male visitors.

The younger children were placed with the Children's Home Society. Mrs. Mallory and her guests were fined for the offense of disorderly conduct. She and her two oldest daughters, Nannie and Jessie, were also held at the City Detention Home. After three weeks there, Mrs. Mallory and her daughters were judged to be feeble-minded and were sent to the Colony.

After six months in the institution, Mrs. Mallory was sterilized by Dr. Priddy. He testified at the trial that the surgery was a medical necessity. Mrs. Mallory testified that there was no illness involved and the only purpose of the surgery was sterilization. Shortly after the operation, she was discharged from the institution. Her daughter Jessie was released soon after, also sterilized.

In October of 1917 George Mallory brought suit against Albert Priddy. Mr. Mallory sought damages for the wages his wife lost during the time she was kept at the Colony, as well as compensation for the pain and suffering caused by her sterilization. He also sought the release of his daughter, Nannie, from the Colony.

Dr. Priddy's testimony that he had admitted Mrs. Mallory to the Colony legally and had sterilized her for *medical* reasons was apparently convincing enough for the jury. On March 1, 1918, a verdict of not guilty was returned in *Mallory v. Priddy*. A number of accounts circulated locally, according to Lombardo, indicate that the judge in the case suggested that Dr. Priddy consider not sterilizing any other patients at the Colony until there was such a law which allowed him to legally do so for eugenic purposes.

The effect of this legal scolding was obviously short-lived. In his 1923 report, Priddy was again referring with pride to the sterilizations he had performed for "medical" reasons at the Colony and the positive effect they had on the overall well-being of women on whom he performed the surgery. Also, the embarrassment was soon to give way to a concentrated push on the part of Priddy, Strode and DeJarnette to secure the passage of an eugenic sterilization law which would survive a constitutional test.

4

Inside The Colony—
Emma, Carrie
and Doris

*T*he Murkland property, initially conceived as the site
for the future hospital, had not ultimately become the
location for the institution. After considering it, the State
Hospital Board decided that it was not adequate for the
purposes of the Epileptic Colony. The General Assembly
authorized the Board to sell the Murkland tract and use
the proceeds toward the purchase of suitable land in a
more convenient area. The Board bought the Willis
Farm, which consisted of 1,000 acres, also on the north
bank of the James River opposite Lynchburg.

It was, therefore, to this facility that a frightened

seventeen-year-old Carrie Buck arrived on a dreary June 4, 1924.

The day after she was admitted, Dr. J. H. Bell, who would later become Superintendent of the Colony and play a prominent role in Carrie's future, examined her. He noted that she was dark and slight, with a low narrow forehead and high cheekbones.

Unlike her mother, who had been admitted in poor health, Carrie's health was generally good. She was well nourished; her body was clean and free from eruptions. The glandular appearance of her abdomen caused Dr. Bell to report that "she'd had a child."

Indeed, it was the birth of this child, Vivian Elaine, and the events which had brought about her pregnancy that had caused Carrie to be committed in the first place.

Carrie was to live in Ward FB9, one of several dormitory-like buildings clustered around the Colony. There were as many as 200 beds in each single-sex dormitory. Anywhere from 700 to 1,000 people were accomodated. Since the Colony was a working farm, raising its own pigs, cows and chickens, as well as fruits and vegetables, each inmate was given a work assignment.

Carrie was assigned kitchen duty.

Chores at the institution began at dawn and lasted well into the night. For Carrie, this meant preparing food, serving it, and cleaning up afterward for the two hundred people in her building. The primitive kitchens were grouped in the open areas of each dorm. Carrie and the other kitchen assistants cooked the simple meals in large, black, iron pots.

The meals were served out on tin cups and plates which rattled noisily as they were placed on the rough hewn tables. Almost as soon as one meal was served, eaten and cleaned up, it was time to begin the preparations for the next.

In the few free moments accorded her, Carrie began to find her way around the other buildings. She knew that her mother lived in one of them. Finally, she found her. Her mother had been assigned to the sewing room in Building V. It was the task of Emma and the others assigned there to sew the clothes needed for the inmates of the Colony. Emma was good at her work.

A note on Emma's chart read: "Patient in good physical health and has not changed mentally. Works well in sewing room and seems perfectly satisfied."

Mother and daughter were comforted by their meetings, but again it was Carrie's assuming her familiar caretaker role which made these visits possible, bringing her mother small treats from the kitchen and news of the world outside. Surprisingly, or perhaps not so surprisingly, in their visits together neither mother nor daughter spoke of the past, but only of the trivial, the mundane.

Not long after arriving, Carrie had begun taking furloughs to the Dobbs home. There, she saw for the first time her child Vivian Elaine.

On December 10, 1927, another member of the Buck family was admitted to the institution, Carrie's half-sister, Doris. But Doris was not to accept her incarceration as docilely as her mother and sister. Though there were strict rules at the institution "about socializing between sexes," Doris rarely obeyed them. Several times she slipped away and was gone overnight, until she finally ran off to elope with her first husband.

Doris was also assigned to kitchen duty as Carrie

ILLUSTRATION 2: Drewry-Gillian Building where Carrie and
Doris Buck lived in open wards on the second floor.

had been—though she took her duties much less seriously and "snuck down to the river as often as possible." Still, despite the difference in their personalities, the sisters became good friends and saw their mother frequently.

Nevertheless, the work was hard and unending. The Buck girls, like most of those in the Colony, dreamed of getting out and "of being free."

Her fearful memories of the Colony remained trapped in Carrie's mind for years after and caused the Newberrys, the family with whom Carrie would be housed when she left the institution, to comment, "She hates the idea of going back to Lynchburg again."

Carrie herself would beg Dr. Bell, the superintendent after Priddy, to give her a discharge rather than a parole from the place she remembered so painfully:

> I hope you will not put it against me and have me come back there. . . . You have promised (the discharge) in a year's time, but I guess the trouble I had will throw me back in getting it, . . . but I hope not.

Six months after her arrival, Dr. Priddy stood as a witness before Aubrey Strode (attorney for the Board), R. G. Shelton (Carrie's guardian) and other members of the Colony Board and gave his opinion of Carrie Buck's mental condition:

I have had Carrie Buck under observation and care in the Colony since the date of her admission on June 4, 1924, and from psychological examination and the Standford revision of the Binet-Simon mental test, I have ascertained that she is feeble-minded of the lowest grade Moron class. Her mental age is nine years, or of the average child at nine years, and her chronological age is eighteen years her last birthday. The sworn history of her case, as shown in the deposition constituting a part of the commitment papers, is that she is of unknown paternity, her mother, Emma Buck, is and has been for several years a feeble-minded patient in the Colony of low mental grade. According to the depositions Carrie has had one illegitimate mentally defective child. She is a moral delinquent but physically capable of earning her own living if protected against childbearing by sterilization. Otherwise she would have to remain in an institution for mentally defectives during the period of her child-bearing potentiality covering thirty years. The history of all such cases in which mental defectiveness, insanity and epilepsy develop in the generations of feeble-minded persons is that the baneful effects of heredity will be shown in descendents of all future generations. Should she be corrected against child-bearing by the simple and comparatively harmless operation of salpingectomy, she could leave the institution, enjoy her liberty and life and become self-sustaining.

In a serious voice, R. G. Shelton asked, "Doctor, what assurance can you give that the operation sug-

ILLUSTRATION 3: Albert Sidney Priddy. Reprinted from
History of Virginia, Vol. V, Virginia Biography. New York: The
American Historical Society. Courtesy of Jones Memorial
Library, Lynchburg, Virginia.

gested by you in this case will not be dangerous to the health, or even the life, of Carrie Buck?"

Priddy disdainfully turned the question aside, "I have performed and assisted in the performance of 90 or 100 operations on female patients in this institution for pelvic diseases involving the removal of diseased tubes which necessarily required sterilization which is a more radical operation in that the tubes themselves are removed, then salpingectomy performed on sound tubes for sterilization, which is simply a division and ligating the Fallopian tubes without any serious consequences whatsoever.

Patients as a rule leave their beds in from two to three weeks and none of their womanly functions are in the least impaired except that of conception and procreation. The operation for salpingectomy is as harmless as any surgical operation can be, and not a single death has occurred in any of the cases so operated on."

Shelton weighted this answer, "Might not this girl Carrie Buck by some course in proper training in your institution, and without this operation, be brought to such sense of responsibility as that she might be restored to society without constraint and harmful effects both to herself and society?"

Priddy rebuffed this idea. "This would be an impossibility, as mental defectiveness, self-control and moral conception are organically lacking (in her) and cannot be supplied by teaching or training, she being congenitally and incurably defective."

Shelton persisted, "If this operation be not performed, do you know of any other way in which this patient might be restored to society?"

"I do not," Priddy replied confidently.

"Are we to understand," Shelton said soberly, "that unless this girl is so operated upon it is likely that both for her protection and the protection of society she must be kept in custody and confinement until her childbearing age is past?"

All eyes fastened on Priddy. His answer left no doubt, "It is necessary that she be kept in custody during the period of childbearing."

With a sigh and a hint of boredom, Aubrey Strode turned to Carrie. "Do you care anything about having this operation performed on you?"

The slight, angular, sharp-featured girl looked at him soberly, pondering the question for several minutes. She seemed surprised that anyone had spoken to her. A silence fell in the room. Then, in the only words she uttered aloud during the entire course of the trial, Carrie said with dignity, "I have not, it is up to my people."

It would have been perfectly normal for Carrie to have assumed that her family would be involved in making the decision of what was best for her. It was a reasonable assumption of trust for her to make: that somehow, someone would look out for her best interests. Tragically, Carrie had no "people" to help her. She was alone.

The Board's conclusion came quickly, declaring that:

> Carrie Buck is a feeble-minded inmate of this institution and by the laws of heredity is the proba-

ble potential parent of socially inadequate offspring likewise afflicted, that she may be sexually sterilized without detriment to her general health, and that the welfare of the said Carrie Buck and of society will be promoted by such sterilization.

Aubrey Strode remembered the atmosphere at the end of the hearing sometime later when he wrote to Don Preston:

> The board then inquired if it might safely proceed under the Act, but I had to advise that the Virginia Act had yet to stand the test of the Courts, where-upon I was instructed to take to court a test case.

By the middle of September, not long after the Board had voted that Carrie Buck should be sexually sterilized by Dr. Priddy, the die had been cast in the selection of Carrie for the test case.

Dr. Priddy immediately began accumulating information. On September 19th he wrote to Caroline Wilhelm asking for her help in collecting background information on Carrie. He reminded Miss Wilhelm that she had not only been responsible for Carrie's admission to the Colony, but her mother's admission as well. Only a day earlier he had written to Miss Edith Furbish of the National Committee for Mental Hygiene, requesting her help in conducting a study of Carrie's heredity. The major assistance in this particular area, however, was eventually to come from Harry Laughlin, who worked for the Eugenics Record Office in Long Island.

Aubrey Strode, the chief administrator of the State Colony and the legislator who had drafted Virginia's sterilization law, himself challenged the right of the State to perform the operation. Years later, following Priddy's death, Strode recalled his original participation introducing the sterilization law:

"Some eighteen years ago, as I recall it, the late Dr. A. S. Priddy, then Superintendent of the Virginia State Colony for Epileptics and Feebleminded, who had shortly before that been sued in a Richmond court for a large amount of damages for having sterilized a feeble-minded woman patient in the Colony, and could successfully defend only on the ground that the operation was indicated for therapeutic purposes rather than eugenically, came to me as counsel for the Colony to convey the request of the State Hospital Board that I examine the question and advise the Board upon the prospect of having the Legislature legally enact that inmates of State Institutions for the Epileptic, Feeble-minded and Insane might, after proper proceedings, be sterilized for eugenical purposes.

In the several states in which the legality of similar enactments had been drawn in question in the courts, in every case that I could find, the Acts had been declared unconstitutional on grounds as being class legislation, if confined in operation to patients in state institutions, as not affording due process of law, if the sterilizing was done without proper previous notice and reasonable opportunity to defend against its need, and as depriving a person of the

49

natural right of procreation beyond the power of the state legally to take away.

So, reporting to the Board, I added that several years before that I recalled that when I was a member of the State Senate, Dr. Carrington, Surgeon to the State Penitentiary, had come before the Committee on Public Institutions to suggest the advisability of legislation to allow the sterilization of selected prisoners, but got no favorable response in the light of public sentiment then existent upon the subject.

The Board for the time dropped the matter so far as I know, but, two years later, Dr. Priddy came back to me to say that the Board, in view of its importance to the institutions, and upon the advice of Governor Trinkle who was interested, requested that I draft a bill for presentation to the Legislature curing such defects as I could in the form of the Acts declared invalid by the courts, trusting that the growth of knowledge of the laws of heredity and eugenics and changing public sentiment might bring a more favorable attitude from the Legislature and the courts.

This, after further study, I did. The bill, at the request of Dr. Priddy and of the State Hospital Board, was introduced by Senator M. B. Booker of Halifax and enacted in 1924, I believe without a dissenting vote, so great had been the change of public sentiment upon the subject . . . I was instructed to take to court a test case. With the very active and helpful cooperation of Doctors A. S. Priddy and J. S. DeJarnette this was done, having as the subject of the litigation Carrie Buck, a typical 19-year-old, feeble-minded patient of the Colony having an illegitimate infant already giving evidence of feeblemindedness, and Carrie's mother also being a feeble-minded patient at the Colony.

Thus we see the intricate and self-motivated origins of the Virginia law on sterilization. The law itself was born out of a perceived eugenic need, but the actual circumstances of its birth had become extremely personal in nature. Aubrey Strode, lawyer, politician, and war hero, was guided in his advocacy by his close personal friend, Albert Priddy. Priddy, a politician himself, suffering from his recent bouts with the courts regarding sterilization, was extremely anxious to legalize efforts he was already making through sterilizations, camouflaging them under the guise of medical necessity. It would be perfectly natural for him to call in favors he had done for Strode and his second wife, Louisa, who had shared with her husband-to-be her admiration for eugenic researcher Arthur Estabrook. Irving Whitehead, supposedly protecting the rights of Carrie Buck, was indeed a childhood friend of Strode's, and even secured for him the military position he held during World War I. All of these characters would continue to play their roles in the drama of compulsory human sterilization.

All that was needed was a person through whom the law could be tried.

5

Prophetic Preliminaries

---

*A*lbemarle County is set apart from other Virginia counties in the Piedmont. In the pre- and post-revolutionary eras the masters of its estates were men of unusual ability and breeding. Thomas Jefferson, by far the best known, is representative of the distinctive class. Many were the products of several generations of advantageous circumstances. Sons of aggressive, self-made, Tidewater gentry flocked to the Piedmont in the mid-1700s to develop tobacco land. They stayed on to grow other crops and discovered in Albemarle a comfortable existence which began to extend upon them a strange charisma which exists for many of their descendants even today.

The men were an intelligent, well-educated, lot. They built great houses appropriate to their extensive lands. Pre-revolutionary homes such as Edgehill Manor, Old Woodville, Edgemont and, of course, Monticello reveal the society they were well designed to serve.

These individuals excelled in agriculture, medicine, surveying, land speculation, politics, the military, theology and the mercantile trades.

Albemarle has long been known as Jefferson's county, named for the most distinguished of the significant men who, by birth, choice or chance, came to live within its boundaries.

About half of the county lies in the Piedmont section and half in what is often called the Middle Virginia region. Stretching from east to west, the elevation varies from 400 to 3161 feet above sea level and there are said to be eighteen different soils, of which the best, Cecil Clay, was first used by the early settlers to grow the tobacco for which colonial Virginia came to be known.

Trapezoid-shaped, Albemarle is bounded by Fluvana and Louisa counties and the James River on the southeast, by Nelson County on the southwest, on the west by the Augusta County line along the crest of the Blue Ridge Mountains and on the north by Greene and Orange counties. This was the region of Carrie Buck's birth and childhood.

Further to the southwest of Albemarle, beyond Nelson County, lies Amherst County. In looking at a map, a traveler sees that most of the main roads and larger towns are in the middle of Amherst county. In the center is the wide and inviting valley which attracted early settlers and in which most contemporary development has occurred.

The village located in the valley, and which was chosen as the county seat, was known in the 1800's as Five Oaks. Eventually it became known as the town of Amherst. The town today is quiet and appealing. Its proud homes and ancient trees give it an almost stereotyped appearance of a small Virginia town. The old white courthouse with its stately facade was built in 1870. It is still used every day for the official and judicial affairs of the people of Amherst. It was in this same courthouse that Carrie Buck's case was first heard.

Before the case began, however, a report was to be submitted to the court by Harry Laughlin.

Harry Laughlin's involvement in Carrie's case was arranged by Strode and Priddy. He was a recognized expert on sterilization and the author of the model sterilization law used in the drafting of Virginia's statute. His disposition in Carrie's case would prove to be influential in the initial hearings, as well as in the appeals, even though there appears to be no evidence that he had ever had direct contact with the people about whom he was making critical judgments.

In an October 7th letter to Priddy, Strode spoke of wanting to send information to Laughlin:

> . . . If you can assist us in getting together as much of the data as possible indicated by him, I shall be glad to forward it together with such questions as Mr. Whitehead and I may agree upon to obtain the desired deposition, all of which should be done as soon as possible if we are to have a hearing at the October Term of the Court.

On October 14th, Priddy answered Strode, indicating that he had complied with his request and forwarded information to Laughlin on Carrie and her family. He stressed that he hoped Laughlin would be able to utilize the information to provide a deposition which would be helpful.

My dear Dr. Laughlin:

My friend and attorney Col. Aubrey E. Strode referred your letter of the 3rd inst. to me relative to your working out (a) genealogical tree and giving depositions in the case of Carrie Buck, a feeble-minded girl in this institution, . . .

When I was instructed by the Governor in our General State Hospital Board, the governing body of the five institutions of Virginia in September of 1923, to prepare and have pushed through the General Assembly of Virginia, a Sterilization Law, I gave Col. Strode all of the information including your book on *Eugenical Sterilization in the United States* which you kindly gave me, and he prepared a bill which the Court of Justice Committee of our Senate, composed altogether of the best lawyers in that body, declared to be an admirable sterilization bill . . . though Dr. J. S. DeJarnette, Superintendent of the Western State Hospital, who has enthusiastically advocated sterilization for years, and myself, fully explained to these lawyers that in our mind, there was grave doubt as to whether a sterilization law could be passed, which would be upheld by the Courts of today; though with a progressive enlightenment as to the needs of eugenics, they might get away from their constitutional moorings within a few years, and give decisions, which would meet this pressing need. It passed both branches of our General Assembly and became law on June 17th, 1924.

I am willing to concede all that opponents of the Sterilization Law claim that they cannot and will not do, but with us in Virginia, it is strictly a humanitarian and economic provision. I conduct the only white institution for mental defectives in Virginia and this State with a population of about 1,600,000 whites, is not financially able without a greatly increased tax rate to care for more than a handful, comparatively speaking, of anti-social women and girls of one hundred counties and twenty cities, who bear illegitimate children, and increase the population of mental defectives to a degree which cannot be calculated in fifty years by any mathematician.

Our purpose is to use, as I have been trying for some ten years, this Institution as a kind of clearing house to give these young women educational, industrial and moral training, sterilize them and send them out to earn their own living, and permit them to enjoy 'Liberty and the peaceful pursuit of happiness' guaranteed in our Declaration of Independence, and to relieve the State of this enormous burden.

Now, as to our test case, I am very sorry I cannot make you out a genealogical tree such as you would like to have, but this girl comes from a shiftless, ignorant and moving class of people, and it is impossible to get intelligent and satisfactory data, though,

I have had Miss Wilhelm, of the Red Cross of Charlottesville, try to work out their line. We have several Bucks and Harlows, but on investigation it is denied that they are any kin to the Harlows, the maternal grandfather of Carrie Buck . . . but the line of baneful heredity seems conclusive and unbroken on the side of her mother (Harlow), but all of the Bucks and Harlows we have here descend from the Bucks and Harlows of Albemarle County in which the City of Charlottesville and the University of Virginia are located and, I believe, they are of the same stock. She has two or three half-brothers and sisters, but at an early age they were taken from the custody of their Mother and legally adopted by people not related to them. All that I can learn about Emma Buck's Father, Richard Harlow, the grandfather of Carrie, (is that he) died from spinal trouble. Carrie Buck, when four years old, was adopted by Mrs. J. T. Dobbs of Charlottesville, who kept her until her moral delinquencies culminated in the illegitimate birth of a child referred to. She attended school five years and attained the 6th grade; she was fairly helpful in the domestic work of the household under strict supervision; so far as I understand, there was no physical development or mental trouble (that) attended her early years. She is well grown, has rather badly formed face, of a sensual emotional nature with a mental age of nine years; is incapable of self support and restraint except under strict supervision.

I am sorry to have to give you such little data on which to work but we will greatly appreciate your taking it and doing the best you can in the form of a deposition, properly executed as quickly as possible as we have to have the case tried in the next Court about the 20th of this month.

If you will kindly send me a bill for the cost incurred in making this deposition, I will send you a check by return mail.

With thanks in advance and kind personal regards, I am,

Sincerely,
A. S. Priddy

In fact, Laughlin used some of Priddy's statements word-for-word in his deposition. Although never having seen Carrie Buck, Laughlin took Priddy's sparse information and produced a deposition as an expert witness. Eventually this information would be accepted by the Courts, even the Supreme Court, as valid testimony and it was clearly influential in the outcome of the case.

In an October 3rd letter to Aubrey Strode about his deposition, Laughlin referred to Carrie's daughter as being feeble-minded, though there seems to be no record that Carrie's child had been medically or psychologically examined at that time. His reference must have been based on his own assumption of deficiency in the child or something that Strode had said or implied. Regardless of the source of this assumption, it was basic to the case being presented that Carrie was the defective child of a defective mother and was in turn the mother of a defective child. This portrait of Carrie as a conduit of human deficiency was the core of the eugenic rationale being presented to the court.

Whether because of his own recognition of the importance of this point or at the urging of Strode or Laughlin, Priddy again wrote to Caroline Wilhelm asking for evidence that Carrie's child was retarded. Miss Wilhelm responded with what must have been a disturbing message to Priddy. After reviewing her Red Cross files she wrote on October 15th:

> My dear Dr. Priddy,
>
> I do not recall and am unable to find any mention in our files of having said that Carrie Buck's baby was mentally defected. In a letter of May 5th, I said that we should not want to take the responsibility of placing so young a child whose mother and grandmother are both mental defectives.
>
> Caroline Wilhelm

These words startled Priddy. In a letter to Dr. J. S. DeJarnette, his friend and the superintendent at Western State Hospital, he conceptualized the case as being focused on Carrie's child and he appealed for DeJarnette's help in bringing the eugenic message to the court.

> Dear DeJarnette:
>
> A special term of the Court of Amherst will be held on Tuesday morning, November 18th, 1924 to hear . . . the case of Carrie Buck, on which the constitutionality of the sterilization law depends. It is abso-

lutely necessary that you be present and I would suggest that you read up all you can on heredity like (the) Jukes, Callikaks [sp.] and other noted families . . .

I am not well enough to go to Charlottesville and have much more than I can do before now and then, I want you to help me in this matter by going over to Charlottesville and calling on Miss Wilhelm, the American Red Cross Nurse in the National Bank Building who will take you around to get a mental test of Carrie Buck's baby which is now from four to five months old.

I am enclosing a letter received from Miss Wilhelm. The test you will make will be the usual one in line with the included test sheet. We are leaving nothing undone in evidence to this case . . . I am enclosing you a letter from Dr. Laughlin and think you will need it. Please return the inclosures [sp.] as Col. Strode may want them for his files, he having had the correspondence with Dr. Laughlin.

We have an advantage in having both Carrie Buck and her mother, Emma, as inmates in this institution.

Priddy's reference to the "Jukes" and "Callikaks" concerned two of the famous family pedigree studies that were often cited as evidence for the need for eugenic measures. Although there were many of these studies of claimed family degeneracy which were used to bolster eugenics arguments (the Jukes and Nams of New York, the Tribe of Ishmael in Indiana, the Hill Folk in Ohio, and the Dacks in Pennsylvania), the most powerful and influential had been reported in 1912 by Henry Goddard in his book *The Killikak Family: A Study in the Heredity of Feeble-Mindedness*. It was that study—its genesis and its legacy—that was the subject of *Minds Made Feeble* by J. David Smith, one of the authors of this book.

Goddard's study was based on the family background of a young girl to whom he gave the pseudonym Deborah Kallikak. She was a resident of the Training School for Feeble-minded Girls and Boys in Vineland, New Jersey. Goddard was convinced that his findings about Deborah, her relatives and her ancestors proved that mental retardation was almost always a matter of genetics—of a "bad seed." Moreover, he interpreted his data on the Kallikak family as evidence that prostitution, alcoholism, criminality, and other social ills were merely by-products of the same genetic flaw that caused retardation. The Kallikak study, along with Goddard's subsequent work and that of many other eugenicists, proved to be a very potent indictment of the poor, the uneducated, social minorities, the foreign born, and those classified as mentally retarded or mentally ill. Eugenics was used by the privileged to justify the naturalness of their privileges—only "good stock" was capable of acquiring and managing power and prerogatives. The "science" of eugenics led to the enactment of more and larger institutions for those persons deemed deficient or defective. Eugenic data was also used by politicians to argue against the expenditure of funds for education, health, and housing for the "bad Kallikaks" of the nation.

According to Goddard:

They were feeble-minded and no amount of education or good environment can change a feeble-minded individual into a normal one, anymore than it can change a red-haired stock into a black-haired stock.

On the same day Dr. Priddy wrote to Dr. DeJarnette, he also wrote to Aubrey Strode concerning preparation for the Circuit Court hearing of Carrie Buck's case. He was obviously concerned that everything be ready for what he saw as being an historic moment.

I am glad that you can get depositions from Dr. Laughlin and I think it very important that Dr. Estabrook attend the trial . . . I want Dr. DeJarnette to stop at Charlottesville and see Carrie Buck's child and note any subnormality of either physical or mental so that he will be prepared to testify. Of course I do not know just what will be allowed in testimony, whether we will be allowed to give the history of criminal immorality, mental defective and diseased union which have billowed in the wake of the lives of the notorious Jukes, Callikaks [sp.] and to the families (to whom) innumerable hundreds of crimes can be traced . . .

6

Old Friends Meet

---

*T*hese events set the stage for the trial of Carrie Buck in the Circuit Court of Amherst County, beginning on the chilly gray morning of November 18, 1924.

The major combatants who appeared in the courtroom that morning to defend, prosecute and judge Carrie Buck were old friends.

Perhaps the most notable was Aubrey Strode, the attorney for Dr. Priddy, the Colony and Virginia. Silver-haired and distinguished, the forty-six-year-old Strode was a prominent Virginia politician.

ILLUSTRATION 4: Aubrey Ellis Strode. Reprinted with permission from the Department of Manuscripts, Alderman Library, University of Virginia.

He was born in 1873 at "Kenmore," his family home in Amherst County. He received his early education at a high school founded and conducted by his father, Professor Henry Aubrey Strode. His mother was Mildred Ellis Strode. Following his father's appointment as the first president of Clemson University he studied there, later at the University of Mississippi, and still later at Washington and Lee University. He taught school for a few years before studying law at the University of Virginia. He opened a law office in Amherst in 1899. He moved his practice to Lynchburg in 1901.

Strode's talents as an orator and legal scholar soon earned him a large clientele. His success and prominence as a lawyer led to his election to three two-year terms in the Virginia State Senate (1906–1910 and 1916–1918). As a State Senator, he earned distinction for himself as an advocate of penal reform and public welfare measures.

Strode also helped draft legislation which established the state health department. He was instrumental in the creation of Virginia's parole and probation system. He authored and sponsored various educational measures, including state loans for needy students in schools and colleges, the establishment of a coordinate college for women with the University of Virginia and the admission of female students to the College of William and Mary.

During World War I Strode closed his law office and accepted a commission as a major in the Judge Advocate General's office. He served in this capacity in both the United States and in France. In France, he was on the staff of General Pershing and was promoted to the rank of lieutenant colonel.

After the war, Strode resumed his law practice. Through his efforts on behalf of prison reform, he became known widely in Virginia as a social activist and humanitarian.

Although he was successful and revered in his public life, Strode privately endured experiences of tragedy and self-doubt which shed light on the reasons for his involvement in eugenics, his interest in the establishment of custodial institutions for the mentally handicapped and, ultimately, his role in the sterilization of Carrie Buck.

In 1902 Aubrey Strode had difficulty securing a life insurance policy. He was only twenty-nine years old and was about to be married to Rebekah Brown. A letter to his family physician, Dr. F. F. Voorheis, explains the reasons for his difficulty and begins to illuminate his interest in mentally handicapped people:

> Dear Doctor:
>
> I have an application for life insurance pending which the company is inclined to reject because both of my parents died in hospitals for the insane. The agent here thinks that an explanation of the facts and circumstances might secure the policy.
> Could you write me a letter stating
> 1) How long you knew my mother and father and how long you were our family physician?
> 2) How long you knew my mother's family and its freedom from insanity?

3) The causes of insanity of both my mother and father?
4) How far in your opinion my insurability should be affected by their insanity?
5) Was their insanity original or merely the symptom of another disease in each case to wit: paralysis causing softening of the brain superinducing insanity in the one case and an abscess producing the same result temporarily in the other case?
6) The general health of my mother and father and of their families?

An early reply will be appreciated.

> Very truly yours,
> Aubrey E. Strode

p.s. Please return this letter with your reply.

Strode also sent similar letters requesting information from the superintendent at Western State Hospital where his father was a patient when he died and from the superintendent at Southwestern State Hospital where his mother died as a patient. The responses he received to these letters offered support for his insurability by presenting his parents as the victims of illnesses that were not hereditary in origin. This information may also have been reassuring to Strode for his own personal confidence. The entire experience of his parents' deaths must have sensitized him to the issue of the hereditary origins of some mental disabilities.

The family physician's response to Strode included the following comments:

1) I have known H. A. Strode and wife for twenty-five years and I was their physician for 15 or 18 years.
2) I have known Mrs. Ellis, the mother of Mrs. Strode for thirty odd years and she is now and ever has been personally free from mental or physical ailments of any description.
3) Mr. H. A. Strode's breakdown began with rupture of a blood vessel in the brain which induced at first partial paresis; this gradually deepened until it ended in almost complete dementia. I have always supposed it was caused by excessive mental work and great anxiety. He was the most vigorous and active man mentally I have ever known, but physically he was rather sluggish, never took much exercise. Mrs. Strode, while Mr. Strode was in above described condition, had a heavy burden thrown on her and was exceedingly anxious and very much worried. At this time she developed a pelvic abscess which was latent as far as symptoms were concerned, not giving the slightest indication of its presence until just before she died. This was the cause of her mental aberration. The abscess burst just before her death (probably a few days) and her mind cleared up completely.
4) I am sure I never had to wait on Mr. and Mrs. Strode for any except trifling ailments during my whole service.

Dr. F. F. Voorheis

Voorheis' letter is interesting, not only for the information it relays concerning Aubrey Strode's parents, but also for the medical opinions of the day that it conveys and implies.

Paul Lombardo has pointed out that Strode, being the eldest son in the family, was probably responsible for committing his parents to the mental institutions where they died. Although we do not know the circumstances and conditions of their commitments, how often he may have visited with them in the hospitals, or the relationships he developed with the staffs of these institutions, this experience must surely have influenced his understanding of and attitudes toward mental disabilities and the public institutions charged with caring for people disabled in this way. This period in his life must also have sensitized him to opinions concerning the hereditary origins of some mental disorders. This may, indeed, have been one important source of his eventually extensive involvement with policies and institutions concerned with people judged to be mentally ill or disabled. The zenith of that involvement occurred with the case of Carrie Buck.

In the summer of 1922, Aubrey Strode's first wife, Rebekah, died in an automobile accident as she was returning from Lynchburg to their Amherst home. This tragedy left him as the single parent of four children and the unaided manager of a home, as well as the principal litigator in a busy law practice. It was a difficult time for him.

By the end of December of the following year, however, Strode was married to his second wife, Louisa Hubbard. He had known Louisa for several years, and the story of their friendship and eventual courtship is interesting in several respects. First, of course, it is part of the saga of Strode's personal life. Secondly, however, it is important because it helps explain further the human relationships which were instrumental in the Carrie Buck case. Finally, the relationship of Aubrey Strode and Louisa Hubbard was seasoned at times by their common interest in eugenics.

In November of 1919 Louisa Hubbard was working as Acting Secretary of the Home Service Department of the American Red Cross in Amherst County. As far as can be determined, the function she served was essentially that of a social worker. She wrote to Aubrey Strode asking that he speak at a meeting of the organization which she referred to as a "Red Cross Roll Call." It is quite understandable that she would be seeking Strode's help in this regard. He was known locally as an orator, and he had recently returned from Europe as an officer of the victorious American troops. Pictures of him at this point in his career show a distinguished, handsome figure at mid-life. His silver hair and chiseled features surely reinforced his impressive presence. In the eyes of his county neighbors he was perceived as a war hero. Louisa asked that he speak particularly on the "accomplishments of the Amherst County boys serving the war . . ."

Perhaps as a result of their conversation at that meeting, or through other contacts, Louisa Hubbard must have come to believe that Aubrey Strode was a generous person and that he would be supportive of the efforts of the Red Cross. The next month she wrote to him again, this time asking the use of his office in Amherst for her work.

My dear Mr. Strode,

The office now used by the Home Service Dept. belongs to Mr. Goodwin and a man has just rented it to open a vulcanizing establishment. Really I'm not sorry because tho usually considered a fresh air fiend, I find that I'm evidently not, at least not to the extent that I need as much ventilation as this room offers. It can not be made comfortably warm. There are several available rooms, but none can be used without a good bit of work being done on the same.

Mr. Schraeder suggested that you might be willing to let me use the little room with stove in your law office here, while you are out of town. Does this request seem very "nervy"? I'll have to have a room that can be made a little more liveable than this one, but I shouldn't imagine we would harm anything, yet there will be the use of the stove and wear of things in general, and unless the plan is perfectly satisfactory to you please don't feel that it's your "duty."

> Very truly yours,
> Louisa D. Hubbard

Strode responded quickly and favorably to Louisa Hubbard's request. In just a few days she was writing again thanking him for his generosity. Her letter also indicates that Strode had given her advice on Amherst and its residents. It appears that he counseled the young social worker, who was originally from Bedford County on the opposite side of Lynchburg, on who to see and how to talk with them.

My dear Mr. Strode,

Your letter of the 16th with the two keys came last week, and I wish to thank you very much for lending the use of your office here until Feb. 1, 1920 to the Home Service Dept. of the Red Cross.

This little room is delightful in every way. Am celebrating my first day here, and it is truly a queer sensation to be perfectly comfortable and warm again!

I shall be very careful about the fire, and sincerely hope and trust that you will have no cause for "regrets" on account of having been generous with your property. The paper over the stove is ripped and inclined to give a "drapery" effect. Not at all repulsive to me, but I feared that possibly you hadn't been here for some time and had forgotten exactly how everything looked!

Had a strange, and long to be remembered, trip from Bellevue to Pedlar Mills by way of Sandidages. Fear it was not as "effective" as it should have been, but as recreation and chance for the study of human characters, I feel that nothing can surpass spending the morning in a country store. Enjoyed knowing your friend Mr. Sutton, and I'm sure your ears must have burned all day from the many nice things he and his wife had to say about you. Surely was glad I had met you! Understand fully why you said "Esq." rather than "Mr." in regard to Mr. Tucker, Prin. of Bellevue High School!

The Christmas tree, at the Alms house, I'm delighted to say, due to the citizens of Amherst, was a great success. Haven't been able to procure necessary data so far to complete my report.

With kindest regards, and very best wishes for a Merry Xmas, I am

Most sincerely yours,
Louisa D. Hubbard

The correspondence between Aubrey Strode and Louisa Hubbard indicates that their friendship continued to grow and that he frequently served as a mentor to her. The more than twenty years of age which separated them, however, did not prevent them from having lively exchanges on social issues which interested both of them. One of these issues was eugenics.

In 1920 Louisa Hubbard moved to Greenville, North Carolina to take an administrative position with the American Red Cross. By this time she had become acquainted with the whole Strode family and she corresponded with both Audrey Strode and his wife. It was with him, however, that she most often discussed her work, her ideas and her concerns. Louisa studied social work at both Sweet Briar College in Amherst and at the University of Pennsylvania. Her notebooks in the Strode Collection at the University of Virginia show that she had been exposed to the basic concepts of eugenics. Through her Sweet Briar connection she had come to know A. H. Estabrook, a field worker from the Eugenics Record Office who would testify at Carrie Buck's sterilization trial. Eugenicists at the Eugenics Record Office located on Long Island, New York, were the most enthusiastic advocates of human sterilization. They lectured and wrote in favor of sterilization on the basis of hereditary research conducted by their office and that done by other eugenicists. Estabrook was collaborating with a sociology professor at Sweet Briar in the study of a racially mixed group of people in Amherst County which they would later use to illustrate the supposed ill effects of "race mixing." The group was referred to at the time, and still is in some quarters, as "Issues" or "Ishys." In January of 1923 Louisa wrote to Strode with a reference to Estabrook and the importance of what he had to say about the "Ishys."

> . . . Dr. Estabrook left Sweet Briar and is again in North Carolina. Theresa Ambler and he have both written me about the trip. I'm sorry that you didn't meet. I was interested greatly by what he had to say about the "Ishys" but will have to tell you about that next time . . .

Louisa apparently spoke to both Estabrook and Strode about a woman in the "Issues" group in whom she had a particular interest. The group referred to by this derogatory term actually consisted of people descended from American Indians who were indigenous to the area. In the correspondence that follows we have deleted the name of the woman who is the focus of discussion.

In February of 1923 Estabrook wrote to Louisa Hubbard from Philadelphia:

> My dear Louisa,
>
> Well, I run up here to take a vacation of a day or so as the roads in Virginny had gotten so bad that

Theresa would not go out on them and I didn't blame her . . .

I must call on (deleted) and see what has affected your life. Do you suppose she will affect my life in the same way! . . .

Written at the bottom and on the back of Estabrook's letter was a note in Louisa's handwriting. The letter and note were sent to Aubrey Strode. The note is revealing of the increasingly personal and teasing nature of Louisa Hubbard's relationship with Strode.

Am sending you these as you will remember possibly our discussion of (deleted). One time you so knowingly and with the look of the "all wise" said, "Child, what do you think you can do with (deleted)?" It was this and many other such things which I could not understand that made me want to study social work. For this reason "Dr. Sol" (Estabrook) speaks of it "affecting my life."

I spoke at the American Legion banquet and oh, Mr. Strode, made a terrible break. "Aubrey"—you would have been much dismayed for me.

> Sweet dreams,
> LDH

In two letters, Estabrook elaborated on his opinions concerning the "Issues" in general and the woman that Louisa knew in particular.

Well, after making a look over the Ishes, I have decided that the socialization of these people is impossible. The only solution is the mating of these people into better stocks and, in view of the attitude in which they are now held by their neighbors, there seems a very small likelihood of that ever taking place. The only out-blood brot [sp.] in is thru illegitimate matings, and these not only few in number but the class of outsiders who mate in here, even spasmodically, is very poor.

I have suggested the trying of industrial education in the school to partially replace the academic but (Mr. Lewis) . . . wants to start it out on a large scale basis by hiring a farmer and getting 75 acres of land, and expecting the Ishy young men to work steadily on the place until trained. I suggested the possibility that they did not have in them the stability to do this but he thought they would do this if given the opportunity. I doubt it.

The second letter illustrates Estabrook's use of, and confidence in, intelligence testing and classification as well as his propensity for seeing mental defectiveness as being transmitted by hereditary means.

. . . On the way we saw (deleted)! Theresa was with me when we stopped at her house! She has one idiot child, two illegitimate and two supposedly legitimate by (deleted). We have visited the mission (an Episcopal Church mission) now three times, and I have tested quite a few of them, none of them showing a mentality above that of an eight year old child; all these were school children.

Written on the back of the first letter fragment is a note in Louisa Hubbard's handwriting. It indicates the degree of confidence she placed in Estabrook's opinion. It appears to have been written to Strode.

This is the final ultimatum of a specialist. At least I feel more satisfied.

Other references in the correspondence between Aubrey Strode and Louisa Hubbard show she obviously respected Arthur Estabrook greatly, and discussed his work and philosophy with Strode on several occasions.

In the Charles Davenport Collection at the American Philosophical Society Library is a 1923 letter from Estabrook to Davenport which describes the Indian group in Amherst and indicates again Estabrook's involvement in Amherst County. Davenport was the Director of the Eugenics Record Office and, therefore, Estabrook's employer.

My dear Dr. Davenport:

Since writing your last letter, I have found quite a bit of data about a very interesting group of people near Amherst, Virginia, an inter-mixture of Indian, negro, and white, who have lived in a segregated region for many generations and are called the "Ishes" because during the Civil War, they were in a territory neither black nor white and they themselves were not classified as either. Hence they were called the "issue" people as there was discussion as to how they should be registered, black or white.

Dr. Pretty [sp.] of the Virginia School for the Feeble Minded knows them, and I have access to the local nurse for the county who knows them well. There is much intermarriage in the group and the only school in the region is a mission school in charge of an Episcopal rector. This region is in the mountains.

. . . I think this Virginia work would interest you as there is the segregation and the intermarriage and the mental defectiveness . . .

The relationship of Aubrey Strode and Louisa Hubbard moved from discussing the work of Estabrook to matters of love. In the summer of 1923 they were making marriage plans.

One obstacle, however, stood in their way. Louisa was concerned that because of previous health problems she might be unable to bear children. She alluded to this concern several times in her letters to Strode. Strode seemed untroubled over the question of children in their marriage but to allay her fears he arranged a medical examination for Louisa. The exam would be performed by his friend, Albert Priddy.

Louisa apparently found this arrangement quite agreeable and was anxious to have the examination done.

. . . I feel that every thing will work out all right if Dr. Priddy will just find out truly I can and that there is not too great a risk. Do please let me know just as soon as you hear anything from him . . .

After the examination, she waited with great anticipation for Priddy's written report.

> . . . Oh—I do hope Dr. Priddy will let us hear from him definitely very soon. Of course we think we know it's all right and are acting accordingly, but dearest man, we must *know* in so far as we can . . .

When Dr. Priddy's report finally arrived, Louisa's joy seems to have been immense.

> You simply can never know the way I wanted you to take me in your arms and just hold me the minute that I finished Dr. Priddy's letter. I'm yours—darling I'm yours!! I love Dr. Priddy more today than I ever have—and he has certainly been splendid and thoughtful in every way, and I just know that he will be one of the best friends that "Col. Strode" and the future Mrs. Aubrey E. Strode have.
>
> I sat down with a dictionary and have reread Dr. Priddy's letter a number of times, and am sending it to you to read. "Assuming that you and Col. Strode love each other"! I like that—guess he's questioning you as long as you were not so frank as I. Maybe he thinks I did the proposing too . . .

With his personal problems solved and his life once more stable, Aubrey Strode was able to turn his full attention back to the causes for which he was a staunch champion.

Strode was a complex and busy man. He was an early advocate of women's rights and he used his influence to create greater opportunities for women in Virginia's system of higher education. As a judge, Strode was active in efforts to improve the segregated facilities for black people in public buildings which existed during his time on the bench. He also worked hard to expand programs for the treatment and care of handicapped people. By every measure he appears to have been a politically constructive and humanitarian oriented person. Most of the causes he supported are admirable ones. He approached the question of compulsory sterilization with the same social philosophy and reformist zeal that he applied to the other "good fights" that he entered. He viewed the sterilization of "defectives" as an expression of social concern for the individuals sterilized as well as for society as a whole.

Also in the courtroom that November morning, seated next to the shy, uncomfortable Carrie Buck, was her attorney, Irving Whitehead. He had been asked to defend Carrie by her guardian, R. G. Shelton. He was also Aubrey Strode's close friend.

Through their childhood Strode and Whitehead had been adventurous boys living on neighboring farms in Amherst. Their friendship continued through law school, committee work and a mutual political commitment to the Democratic Party. Even when Whitehead's law practice led him away from Amherst, and he served as counsel for the Federal Land Bank of Baltimore, he and Strode had maintained a mutual correspondence.

During World War I, Whitehead was willing to use his political influence to help his friend secure an Army commission. He spoke several times with Congressman Henry Flood of Virginia. Flood and his brother-in-law, Richard Byrd, eventually established the Byrd political dynasty in Virginia. Flood was chairman, at that time, of the Committee on Foreign Affairs in the United States House of Representatives. These conversations culminated in the letter which Flood sent to Strode on April 10, 1918.

Dear Aubrey:

I telephoned to Irving Whitehead a few days ago, and asked him if you would care for an appointment in the Judge Advocate General's office with the rank of Major. I told Irving I was not positive that I could secure this appointment, though at the time I telephoned him Senator Martin had been positively assured that if we named a competent man, he would be appointed, but knowing the War Department as I did, I thought best to state to Irving that the matter was not absolutely certain. I never like to count on anything from the War Department until I actually have it. I make this brief statement so that you can fully understand the situation.

. . . The position pays $3,000 a year salary, and $60 a month commutation while you are stationed in Washington, and under a bill which passed the House yesterday, and which has already passed the

Senate, and I have no doubt will soon be made law, you would receive this $60 commutation whether you were in Washington or in the field.

I received a telegram from Irving Whitehead saying you would accept the position, and telling me to communicate with you. I would have written to you sooner, but for the fact that these uncertainties which I have written you arose after Colonel Spiller changed his desk in the office of the Judge Advocate General. I feel now that the position will be offered you in a short while, and I have no doubt you could render the Government splendid service, and that you would fine [sp.] the work congenial and useful.

Let me hear from you as soon as you get this. I will keep pushing this matter.

Sincerely yours,
H. D. Flood

After receiving his commission as Judge Advocate Major, Aubrey Strode went to Washington to express his appreciation to Irving Whitehead. Unfortunately, Whitehead had been called away on business, but not long afterward Whitehead wrote his friend.

It was such a good thing we should keep it in the family, and I about made up my mind if you turned it down I would take it myself.

The bond between the two men was to last a lifetime. When Whitehead died on January 20, 1938, the Virginia Bar Association, of which he had been Chairman, asked his wife for a biography of his life to be published in their Journal. She asked his good friend, Aubrey Strode, to write the tribute. Strode wrote:

Few men had a larger personal acquaintance with lawyers throughout the country than he. Upon his death a multitude of tributes to him came from widespread sections bearing testimony to his character, capacity and attainments, and to his loveable personal traits of courage, fidelity and charm. Typical among these a Floridian wrote of "the bigness of his heart and the nobility of his soul"; one United States Senator had "never known a finer man or more loyal friend"; another expressed "deepest sympathy shared by a host of friends and the public which he served so faithfully." From Kentucky came: "Marveled at his grasp of the fundamental principles of the law, his courage, . . . with and good humor . . . one of the sweetest and nicest of souls." And Delaware: "Deepest sympathy." California: "Charming personality and learning in the law." Kansas: "Wonderfully keen and analytical mind, a practical viewpoint, the ability to understand men and a most kindly and sympathetic heart." South Carolina: "A good friend and outstanding counselor." Puerto Rico: "Able adviser." Pennsylvania: "Loved and honored him." Texas: "Rendered great service to the Farm Loan System." West Virginia: "Fine lawyer and loyal friend."

Fortunate indeed were those who were served by and had the friendship of Irving Whitehead, always distinguished by loyalty and devotion.

Most of Whitehead's career was spent specializing in law concerned with the National Farm Loan Policy, and he held jobs as Counsel to the Federal Intermediate Credit Bank and as General Counsel to the Farm Credit Administration. In early 1924 Aubrey Strode had recommended Whitehead for a government job, saying:

> Knowing and esteeming him as I do, I wish to take the liberty . . . of commending him to your favorable consideration.

Both men shared a commitment to the Virginia Colony for Epileptics and the Feebleminded. Strode had taken part in the early organization of the institution, and Whitehead was a member of its first Board of Directors. From the beginning, Strode had written bills both for the benefit of the institution and for the feebleminded. Whitehead represented the Colony to the State Board of Hospitals, and, only recently, a building had been named after him.

When Strode decided to prosecute the Carrie Buck case in the Amherst Circuit Court in order to test Virginia's sterilization law, it was Irving Whitehead who was chosen to represent Carrie Buck in the "friendly" litigation.

Neither before, during or after the trial did anyone question whether Irving Whitehead's ability to act as advocate for Carrie Buck was compromised by his close relationship to those who stood to gain the most from her successful prosectuion. Nor did anyone know or care that shortly after the case was heard, State Colony Superintendent Albert Priddy wrote to Irving Whitehead and sent him payment for his legal services. They were still waiting for the judge to announce his decision.

> I hope very much that Judge Gordon will sustain the law and I am inclined to believe he will.
> I still continue very unwell and though I have been feeling better this week than for sometime, I had a little spell of coughing Tuesday night and as a result of it, one of my vocal chords has since refused to work and on the advice of Drs. Morrison and Gorman, I am going to Philadelphia Sunday to have Dr. Schevelier Jackson examine me. He being considered to be the best laryngologist in the world. I am awfully depressed and discouraged about my condition.
> . . . I am inclosing [sp.] your Institution check for $250.00 in payment of your fees for representing . . . Carrie Buck thro [sp.] the Circuit Court of Amherst.
> With best wishes and kind regards to you and Mrs. Whitehead.
>
> Albert Priddy

Presiding over the courtroom in the matter of *Buck vs. Priddy* was Judge Bennett Gordon, who had known both Strode and Whitehead as boys and as young lawyers practicing in Amherst.

After calling the court to order, Gordon recognized the bald and portly Irving Whitehead, who announced:

Have the record show that the appellant (Carrie's guardian, R. G. Shelton) is present. I want the record to show that the parties are all here.

On this ominous note proclaiming the procedural correctness of the group assembled to decide the fate of Carrie Buck, Whitehead yielded to Aubrey Strode and the trial began.

"If your honor please," Strode stated in his sonorous voice, "we have a number of witnesses here from a distance, including from the counties of Albemarle and Charlottesville, where this girl came from, and, while it would not be done ordinarily, I am going to put them on first in order to allow them to get through and leave for their homes."

"All right, sir," Judge Gordon answered soberly.

Strode looked around the room, "I am going to ask that the witnesses be excluded except Dr. DeJarnette."

The bailiff led the chattering group from the court-room and Strode called to the stand his first witness, Anne Harris, a Charlottesville nurse.

7

The Trial: Neighborly Witnesses

Suave and poised, Colonel Strode slowly moved toward the witness stand, "Mrs. Harris, where do you live?"

"Charlottesville, Virginia."

"Are you engaged in any work there?" Strode asked politely.

"Yes, sir, I was District Nurse there for eleven years," her voice was almost too soft to hear.

Strode leaned toward her and repeated, "You were District Nurse there for eleven years?"

"Yes, sir," she said.

He inquired, "Do you know Carrie Buck?"

"Yes, sir."

Nodding, Strode continued, "The girl involved in this proceeding?"

"Yes, sir."

He was ready now, "How long have you known her?"

"Well, I have known her for probably twelve years."

"Do you know her mother, Emma Buck?"

"Yes, sir."

"How long have you known her?"

"The same length of time."

"What do you know about them, Mrs. Harris?"

"Well, I know . . ."

Mr. Whitehead suddenly interrupted, "Wait a minute, right there is what I think is one of the important features. I am not objecting right now, but I think I will ask later to strike that out because I think that question violates the constitutional right of the defendant."

Shaken by the interruption, Mrs. Harris went on slowly, "Well, I know that Emma Buck, Carrie Buck's mother, was on the charity lists for a number of years, off and on—mostly on; that she was living in the worst neighborhoods, and that she was not able to, or would not, work and support her children, and that they were on the streets more or less."

Strode asked politely, "Do you know any other of the children of Emma Buck besides Carrie?"

"I know a small child, Doris—a girl."

Strode was becoming exasperated. The testimony was taking too long and eliciting little except what was already known, that the Bucks were poor and Carrie's mother was irresponsible.

"Mrs. Harris, we want to make this as brief as

possible, but at the same time, we do want the facts. You have given a very clear-cut and exceedingly short account of these people. Could you not elaborate it in any way? Cannot you tell us more facts about Emma and Carrie? What sort of people were they?

Harris complied, "Well, Emma was absolutely irresponsible. She did not have any idea of providing for herself and children. She was literally on the streets with her children, and the numerous charity organizations worked for her at different times, but all that was done for her was to give her relief."

Strode pressed for more, "Can't you tell us what the trouble was with her?"

"Well, she didn't seem to be able to take care of herself. She would not work. She had these children, and she was not living with her children and she did not take care of them or herself."

"You speak of her not living with her husband: did she continue to have children in spite of that fact?"

Harris nodded, "Yes, sir."

Strode continued, "Were they her husband's children?"

"No, sir. No question of them being her husband's!"

He tried a different tactic, "Are you acquainted with the term used in this statute, 'the socially inadequate person'?"

"Yes, sir."

"What is your idea of that term?"

"A person who is not able to take care of themselves—who is irresponsible mentally."

"Now, you say she is irresponsible mentally?"

"Yes. She is not mentally able to do things or to judge for herself."

"But physically able to bear children?"

"Yes, sir, and to work for her living, but mentally unable to do so."

Strode gave a half smile, "What about the character of her off-spring? I am speaking of Emma now. Do you know anything of the character of her off-spring?"

"Well, I don't know anything very definite about the children, except they don't seem to be able to do any more than their mother."

Strode was now satisfied, "Well, that is the crux of this matter. Are they mentally normal children?"

"No, sir, they are not," Mrs. Harris answered slowly.

He pressed on, "Emma herself was not normal, and they are not?"

"No, sir."

"We have not yet used the term 'feeble-minded'; I was hoping you might get to it yourself. Are you acquainted with that term?"

"Yes, sir."

"I wish you would state whether or not Emma or any of her children were feeble-minded."

Mrs. Harris paused for a moment and then said, "I would say Emma had the mentality of a child of twelve."

"That is the mother of these children?"

"Yes, sir, and the children less than that—certainly of a child four or five years younger than her age."

"Now, you said that you knew Doris?"

"Yes, sir."

"Was she a full sister of Carrie?"

"I should say not, just from hearsay. I don't know definitely, but I should say not, from general reports."

"What was her relationship to Carrie?"

"Well, she was Carrie's half-sister; same mother, but not the same father."

"What do you know about Doris?"

"Well, she was a very stormy individual. She was a very violent child. She ruled her mother before she was placed in the children's home. She was with some people in the country, and they had a very stormy time with her, and they could not do anything with her. She had an ungovernable temper. She was incorrigible."

Mr. Whitehead interrupted again, "Without waiving my right to move to strike out all of it, I ask two or three questions." On his cross-examination, Whitehead was a less courtly figure than Strode, but no less intelligent, "Mrs. Harris, you speak of Doris: Doris is a half-sister of the girl that is here, Carrie Buck?"

"Yes, sir, supposed to be . . ."

Whitehead succinctly made his point, "Now, of course you don't know whether she is a half-sister or not, do you?"

"No, sir, I do not know who the child's father was."

Looking toward the judge, Whitehead asked, "The record you have given of the mother, Emma Buck, that is made up on what you have heard, largely?" He turned back to the witness.

"No, sir," Mrs. Harris insisted, "I had her on my list for years."

"She was a married woman?"

"Yes, sir."

"Her husband was not living with her?"

"No, sir."

"Is Carrie, the girl here, supposed to be his legitimate child?"

"No, sir, she is illegitimate."

Whitehead pressed, "Was Carrie born while her mother was living with her husband?"

Mrs. Harris shook her head, "No, sir.'

"Then her husband must not have lived with her very long?"

"No, sir."

"Where did her husband live?"

"In Charlottesville."

"Of course you don't know whether he visited her?"

"I could not definitely say no."

Whitehead leaned toward the witness questioningly, "Now what are the—what about this girl, Carrie, herself—is there anything about her? Is she incorrigible?"

Mrs. Harris was silent for a moment, "I really know very little about Carrie after she left her mother. Before that time she was most too small."

"She was taken by . . ." Whitehead interrupted.

"She was taken by Mr. and Mrs. Dobbs," Harris explained.

"So far as you know, you know nothing about her after the Dobbs took her?"

Mrs. Harris gave a half-smile, "Except one time when she was in school, in the grammar grade, the Superintendent called me and said she was having trouble with Carrie. She told me that Carrie was writing notes, and that sort of thing, and asked what should she do about it."

"Writing notes to boys, I suppose?"

"Yes, sir."

"Is writing notes to boys in school, nine or ten years old, considered anti-social?"

"It depends on the character of the note."

"Did you see the notes?"

"Yes, sir."

"Well, if the note is not altogether proper, is it evidence of anti-social . . ."

Mrs. Harris was adamant, "For a child ten years old to write the notes she was writing, I should say so."

"Suppose the child had been sixteen years old, would it have been regarded as anti-social for writing that class of notes?"

"I should say so, assuredly."

"Well, then, there is nothing in the age of the child . . . I mean the actual age . . . I ask you, if the child had been sixteen years old, would it still have been anti-social?"

Mrs. Harris' back fairly bristled, "Well, if a girl of sixteen had written that kind of note, she ought to have been sent to Parnell—Isle of Hope."

"Has it come under your observation in your official capacity, any of this girl's own acts?"

"No, sir, not since the Dobbs took her."

On redirect, Strode asked several questions about a distant relative of Carrie's, and, when these produced little relevant information, permitted Mrs. Harris to step down after Whitehead's recross.

The testimony Strode had finally solicited from Mrs. Harris was important in that it set the stage for his

characterization of the Buck family as economically poverty-stricken, sexually promiscuous and mentally retarded.

The three school teachers who followed Harris to the
witness stand continued to flesh out this portrayal.

The first, Eula Wood, testified that Doris Buck, Carrie's half-sister, was slow and had to be held back in
school.

"She is in the first now. She was in the second, and I
put her back."

Strode asked innocently, "Why did you do that?"

Miss Wood replied, "I suggested it; I really didn't do
it myself. The Supervisor put her back."

Strode dropped his voice, "Won't you tell us why it
was done?"

Miss Wood complied, "Well, she couldn't keep up
with the second grade work."

Interrupting, Strode queried, "She couldn't keep up
with the second grade work, although she had been in
school six years?"

"Yes, sir."

"How old is Doris?"

"Eleven or twelve."

Strode pondered the answer for a moment and said
slowly, "Eleven or twelve, and still in the first grade in
school?"

Wood repeated, "Still in the first grade."

"Would you call her a bright child?" Strode asked.

"No," came the obvious reply.

He pushed even further, "Would you call her a dull
child?"

Miss Wood looked as if she preferred not to answer

the question, but finally admitted, "Well, she is dull in her books . . . I would call her dull in her books."

The next testimony by Virginia Beard concentrated on Roy Smith, Carrie's half-brother.

Strode began to build his characterization, "About how old is Roy?"

"Fourteen."

Strode repeated, "He is fourteen. What sort of boy is he at school?

Miss Beard spoke shyly, "Well, he didn't do passing work in the fourth grade."

The answer was not what Strode had wanted. "What sort of behavior has he?" he inquired.

"Well, he tried to be funny—tried to be smart."

Seemingly turning to a different subject, Strode continued, "How does he compare mentally with other boys of his age in school?"

"Well, he is below the grade of other boys of his age in the school," Miss Beard supplied.

Thinking he was close to gaining the response he wanted, Strode pushed too fast, "Basing your reply on your experience as a school teacher, would you consider him weak-minded?"

But Miss Beard disappointed him, "Well, I don't know."

The last teacher to testify was Virginia Landis, who readily admitted at the beginning of her testimony, "I don't know anything about Carric Buck." However, she continued to add to the picture of Carrie's family as mentally defective by discussing George Dudley, Carrie's cousin.

"George attended my school," she supplied, "and I would consider him a dull child, but a normal child."

"How old is he?" asked Strode.

Landis thought for a moment, "George told me he was eleven, but he was very much overgrown for eleven years old. Now, he has not been in my school for two years."

"Why do you say he is both a dull boy and a normal child?"

"Well, we grade them as normal, dull and bright, and I class him with the dull-minded."

"What evidence does he give of being dull?"

"He is slow grasping things in school."

"How was he up on his grades?"

"He was below the average. He was in the fifth grade when he left school."

"What was his age then?"

"He told me eleven, but I heard from other people he was older than that."

"Do you know George's brother, Arthur?"

"Just to speak to him when I see him."

"What do you know about him?"

"Just enough to say 'Good morning' to him."

"You say you know nothing of Arthur except to speak to him?"

"Well, I have met him a few times, but I would not say I was acquainted with him. We would have some little entertainments at school and he would come and stand around, but I had no contact whatever with him. We would just speak to him."

Despite Irving Whitehead's final question, "Do you know what relation, if any, George and Arthur Dudley are to Carrie Buck?" and Landis' reply, "I don't know Carrie Buck at all," Aubrey Strode's message was becoming loud and clear and seemed to be having the desired effect.

John Hopkins, the Superintendent of the Albemarle County Home, a facility for orphans, fortified this message by reporting that Carrie's half-brother, Roy, "was rather an unusual boy."

"In what way?" Strode questioned.

"He struck me as being right peculiar."

Strode reaffirmed the statement, "He is a peculiar boy?"

"I think so."

Strode inquired politely, "Now, why can't you tell us what you know about him?"

Hopkins looked around the room, "Well, the only thing I know that can cause me to have an opinion about him at all is, he came through the place one day—he was going to school. He stopped and was waiting on the path, and I asked him who he was waiting for. He said he was waiting on some other children, they were going home to spend the night with him. I said, 'Boy, those children have gone home.' And he said, 'Well, they was coming with him tomorrow night.' He had been standing there waiting I suppose twenty or thirty minutes . . ."

"Did you tell Dr. Estabrook that you would consider that boy mentally defective and foolish?"

"I think so, yes." Hopkins stammered.

Exasperated, Strode inquired, "Then why don't you tell us, Mr. Hopkins. Are you adverse to testifying?"

"No, sir, but that is all I know about him."

"Now, why do you consider him mentally defective?"

"Well, that is the only thing I ever saw . . ."

"Is that the only time you saw him?"

"No, sir, I have seen him a number of times."

"But, in your opinion, he is mentally defective?"

"Yes, sir, but I can't recall any other specific instance that would cause me to think so—not any particular thing."

Strode took a different approach, "Do you know Richard Dudley?"

"Yes."

"Do you know Carrie Buck?"

"No, sir."

"Do you know Emma Buck, the mother of Carrie?"

"No, sir."

"But you do know Richard."

"Dudley? Yes, sir."

"What do you know about Richard Dudley?"

"Well, I don't know very much about Mr. Dudley. He strikes me as being right peculiar, and that is all I do know about him, but as to why, I couldn't tell you any particular case at all."

"Is he a man above or below the average intelligence?"

"Well, I don't know, sir. I don't know whether I am capable of judging that."

"How far does he live from you, Mr. Hopkins?"

"About half a mile."

"Lives there in the same neighborhood, and you don't know anything about him?" Strode was obviously vexed.

The Trial: Neighborly Witnesses

"I don't see him once in six months," Hopkins replied patiently.

Annoyed, Strode continued, "Didn't you tell Dr. Estabrook yesterday . . ."

Mr. Hopkins finally broke, "I did—I told him I thought so, but since considering that thing. . . ."

Strode calmed him down, "It is natural that it would be embarrassing to you to testify about these people— being neighbors."

"I know, but I don't mind telling you, what I know to be a fact."

Strode changed directions, "Do you know Richard's son, Arthur?"

"Yes, sir."

"What do you know about him?"

"Well, he has always struck me as being a little peculiar. Now, the only instance I can recall, I had an engine that wouldn't start, and he wanted to try to start it. I knew what was the matter with the engine, but I told him to go ahead if he wanted to do it, and he cranked and cranked, and could not start it, and he told me he had found out what was the matter with the engine; that it wasn't made right."

Strode was getting impatient, "Do you consider him above or below the average?"

"Well, that question is exactly like the other, and I answer it the same way."

Strode was at his wit's end, "Yesterday you thought he was below, and today you don't know?"

Hopkins was no help at all, "Well, I don't know. That is right."

Whitehead began his cross examination quietly, "Do you know the people pretty generally in that neighborhood in which this fellow, Richard Dudley, lives?"

"Yes, sir."

"How far does he live from your place?"

"Half a mile."

"How long have you lived there?"

"Eight years."

"Do you know the people generally around there pretty well, in that neighborhood?"

"Yes, sir."

"What does Richard Dudley do?"

"Well, he has a farm, but he has been working on the section (railroad) for the last two years, I think. I don't know just what he is doing now. I haven't seen him for six or eight months."

"Has he, to your knowledge, ever been guilty of any theft, or anything of that sort?"

"No, sir, never heard a word of harm about him in my life."

"Now, according to your view, is he an average citizen in that neighborhood?"

"Well, take it in that neighborhood, I believe he is."

"Well, what is the matter with the neighborhood?"

"I don't know."

Even Whitehead was beginning to get impatient, "Take it in the neighborhood—is that a neighborhood where all the Sprouses live?"

"Yes, sir. . . . not all of them."

"Is that in the Ragged Mountain of Albemarle?"

"Yes, sir."

"Are the citizens in that neighborhood average citizens of Albemarle, mentally?"

"I don't know. I don't think so."

As Hopkins stepped down, Strode looked out of patience. Whitehead himself seemed a little confused.

Samuel Dudley was another neighbor called to the trial. As it turned out, much to Strode's and Estabrook's surprise, he was also Carrie's great-uncle. He was asked to make comments concerning Carrie's grandfather, Richard Harlow.

He described Richard Harlow, Emma Buck's father, as having "just as good ordinary sense as the generality of people." He finally admitted that he had told one of the expert witnesses, Estabrook, that Richard Harlow was peculiar, or at least "that he had these peculiar ways."

Strode began hesitantly, "What did you . . . What was your opinion of Richard, mentally?"

"Now, Mr. Strode, he wasn't a through educated man. He had some little joking ways sometimes, but outside of that he was all right."

"Did you regard him as at all peculiar in any way?"

"No, no more than just in a joking manner, sir."

"Didn't you tell Dr. Estabrook yesterday or the day before, that you considered Richard peculiar, or below the average?"

"No, sir, I just told him that he had those peculiar ways. That gentleman there (pointing to Estabrook) asked me Saturday night, and pressed me about a lot of things I didn't know anything about."

"Didn't you tell him you thought Richard was peculiar or below the average?"

"Just in this joking ways and the manner he had. He was a man that transacted his own business up until his death."

Strode was beginning to anger, "But you did tell Dr. Estabrook he was peculiar."

Dudley was just as adamant, "Well, possibly I did. He kept quizzing me about different things, and I thought I would just let him go."

"What has become of Richard?"

"Oh, he is dead."

"What was your relationship to him?"

"He married my sister."

The answer had taken Strode by surprise, "He married your sister?"

"Yes," Dudley seemed quite pleased with himself.

Strode decided that another line of questioning might be better, "Do you know anything about the brothers of Richard?"

But Dudley was not much help, "No, I know them when I see them. They live there in Charlottesville."

Things were clearly not going the way Strode had planned. Under cross examination, Dudley made it even clearer that he had no knowledge of Carrie Buck.

"Do you know anything about this little girl here?" Whitehead asked, pointing to Carrie.

Dudley replied, "No, sir, the only thing that I know, they got her in with a family by the name of Dobbs. I never saw the child before in my life."

The next witness, Miss Caroline Wilhelm, the social worker with whom Strode had corresponded, probably came closest to disclosing the truth of Carrie Buck's case. It is unlikely that Carrie would have been institutionalized if she had not gotten pregnant and had an illegitimate child. The combination of her poverty, lack of a protecting family group, limited education and skills, her youth and her pregnancy resulted in her commitment to the State Colony. Her foster family initiated the procedure to institutionalize her only when they discovered that she was pregnant. Had there been some means for her to hide, explain or legitimize her condition, Carrie Buck would not have been classified as feeble-minded. Nor would she have become the victim of and the precedent for compulsory sterilization. Miss Wilhelm's statements demonstrate the circular and inescapable reasoning that led to Carrie's separation from society and her eventual sterilization.

Strode began genially, "Miss Wilhelm, what is your occupation?"

Miss Wilhelm was prepared to be cooperative and friendly, "I am a social worker of the Red Cross. Secretary Superintendent of public welfare of Albemarle County."

"Have you any record of this girl, Carrie Buck?"

"Yes, sir."

"What is her record?"

"I came to Charlottesville about February of this year, and just before that time the case had been reported to Miss Duke, who was in charge temporarily in the office as Secretary, that Mr. Dobbs, who had charge of the girl, had taken her when a small child, had reported to Miss Duke that the girl was pregnant and that he wanted to have her committed somewhere . . . to have her sent to some institution, and wanted Miss Duke to have that brought about. The matter was not put through until I was in the office, and officially I brought Carrie Buck over to the Colony at Lynchburg."

Strode nodded, satisfied with the answer, "You know that Carrie was not married."

Wilhelm replied tautly, "No, she was not."

Strode looked up, "Was that child born?"

"Yes, sir."

Strode persisted, "She had an illegitimate child?"

"Yes, sir," Miss Wilhelm said quietly.

Strode raised his voice, "And her character was such that you had her committed to the institution at Lynchburg?"

Wilhelm appeared uncomfortable, "Yes, sir. There was a commission held and she was committed to the Colony."

Strode's voice became more decisive, "From your experience as a social worker, if Carrie were discharged from the Colony still capable of child-bearing, is she likely to become the parent of deficient off-spring?"

She answered without hesitation, "I should judge so. I think a girl of her mentality is more or less at the mercy of other people, and this girl particularly, from her past record. Her mother had three illegitimate children, and I should say that Carrie would be very likely to have illegitimate children."

Strode nodded affirmatively, "So that the only way that she could likely be kept from increasing her own kind would be by either segregation or something that would stop her power to propagate. Is she an asset or a liability to society?"

She shrugged, "A distinct liability, I should say."

Strode continued, "Did you have any personal dealings with Carrie?"

"Just in the few weeks between the time when the commission was held and when I brought her to Lynchburg."

"Was she obviously feeble-minded?"

"I should say so, as a social worker."

It was this distinction, her professional expertise, which would carry extra weight.

Strode paused, considering, "Did you know her mother?"

"No, I never saw her mother."

Then Strode began to question her about Carrie's illegitimate child, "Where is the child?"

"The child is with Mr. and Mrs. Dobbs. They kept the child."

"How old is the child?"

"It is not quite eight months old."

"Have you any impression about the child?"

"It is difficult to judge probabilities of a child as young as that," she said crisply, "but it seems to me not quite a normal baby."

Strode weighed what she had said carefully and then emphasized the conclusion she had reached, "You don't regard her child as a normal baby?"

She hesitated, then went on, "In its appearance—I should say that perhaps my knowledge of the mother may prejudice me in that regard—But I saw the child at the same time as Mrs. Dobbs' daughter's baby, which is only three days older than this one, and there is a very decided difference in the development of the babies. That was about two weeks ago."

Strode persisted, "You would not judge the child as a normal baby?"

Miss Wilhelm declared thoughtfully, "There is a look about it that is not quite normal, but just what it is, I can't tell."

Mr. Whitehead began his cross-examination also asking about the baby, "This baby you are talking about now is Carrie Buck's baby?"

"Yes, sir."

"What other baby was the comparison made by?"

"Mr. and Mrs. Dobbs', who have had Carrie since she was three years old. They have a daughter who has a baby three days older than Carrie's."

Whitehead's brow creased, "You say the baby of Carrie does not measure up to the Dobbs'?"

"Not nearly."

"Neither one of them can talk?"

"No."

"Can they walk?"

"No."

He grew exasperated, "In what way do they differ?"

She blushed slightly and continued, "Mrs. Dobbs' daughter's baby is a very responsive baby. When you play with it, or try to attract its attention. . . . it is a baby that you can play with. The other baby is not. It seems very apathetic and not responsive."

Whitehead continued politely, "Now, Miss Wilhelm, the only—I want to get at your view about this—you say when this girl first came under your attention she was pregnant?"

"Yes, sir."

"Did you have the commission?"

"No, that was held before I came to Charlottesville."

"You had nothing to do with the commission that adjudged her feeble-minded?"

She seemed uncomfortable, "No."

"When you first knew her she was pregnant, and after that, you sent her to the Colony?"

"Yes, sir. There was some delay about sending her to the Colony.

Whitehead continued questioning, "Now, there are records down in Charlottesville in connection with social work—have they any records against Carrie Buck, the girl here, which would tend to show that she was feeble-minded or unsocial or anti-social, or whatever the term is, other than the birth of this child?"

"No, sir, our record begins on the 17th of January of this year, and that is the first knowledge we have of her."

He seemed dubious about the hastiness of her conclusion, "Basing your opinion that the girl is unsocial, or anti-social, on the fact that she had an illegitimate child—the point I am getting at is this—are you basing your opinion on that?"

But Miss Wilhelm persisted, "On that fact, and that as a social worker I know that girls of that type. . . ."

Whitehead gave a small, tight smile, "Now, what is the type?"

"I should say, decidedly feeble-minded."

"But the question of pregnancy is not evidence of feeblemindedness, is it? The fact that, as we say, she made a miss-step—went wrong—is that evidence of feeble-mindedness?"

"No, but a feeble-minded girl is much more likely to go wrong."

"Now, Miss Wilhelm, there is one more question: you said in answer to Col. Strode that the girl was a decided liability. Do you mean—this girl was taken care of by Mr. Dobbs and his family?"

"Yes, sir."

"Up to the time she gave birth to this child?"

"Yes, sir."

"Up to the time she was removed to the Colony was she still living with the Dobbs?"

"Yes, sir."

"Was she able to do the average work of a girl of her age?"

"Under direction," Miss Wilhelm was not about to be led down the wrong path, "Mrs. Dobbs tells me she needed very careful supervision."

"Under supervision she was able to do household work?"

"Yes, sir."

Whitehead said calmly, but with a slight edge to his voice, "She is a liability. In what way do you think by sterilizing she would become an asset to the State?"

Miss Wilhelm retorted, "I don't know that she would become an asset, but much less of a liability."

Whitehead drew back, "Do you think she could be with safety discharged without being sterilized?"

"I don't know so much about the working of that law and the working out in individual cases. I don't know what the results have been in those cases."

"Now this girl, according to your viewpoint, she has an immoral tendency?" he stated quietly.

KITPLANES®

YES, I want to subscribe to the "Worlds #1 Home built Aircraft Magazine

☐ **$29.95 — 12 monthly issues**
(I save over $17 off the newsstand price.)

☐ **Bill me** (US & Canada only)
Charge my ☐ VISA ☐ MasterCard

Account # _____

Exp. Date _____

Signature _____

My Name _____

Address _____

City/State/Zip _____

Canada add $12/year (postage & GST); Foreign add $12/year surface mail or
$45/year air delivery. International money order, please.

Please allow 6 to 8 weeks for delivery

Save Up To $17

6R94A1

BUSINESS REPLY MAIL

FIRST-CLASS MAIL   PERMIT NO. 40   FLAGLER BEACH FL

POSTAGE WILL BE PAID BY ADDRESSEE

KITPLANES®

SUBSCRIPTION DEPT.
PO BOX 420264
PALM COAST FL 32142-9532

"Certainly," she snapped back.

He continued, "Judging by the fact that she has already given birth to an illegimate child, and has an immoral tendency, is it your opinion that by sterilization she would be made less of a liability and more of an asset to the State?"

Wilhelm glared, "I think it would at least prevent the propagation of her kind."

Amid the quiet in the room, Whitehead opined, "It would prevent the propagation of her kind, undoubtedly, but is it your opinion that it would have a deterrent effect in that it would make her less immoral?"

Her voice drifted off, "I am afraid I am not competent to judge of that."

He paused again and then stated, "Your idea is, while she would never become an asset, she would become less of a liability by sterilization, and your idea is that she could be turned over to somebody and, under careful supervision, be made self-supporting. Is that your idea?"

"I think so, yes, sir."

With this, Whitehead concluded.

Mary Duke, the eighth and last witness from Charlottesville, had been in charge of social work until Miss Wilhelm had taken over. In that position, she knew Emma Buck.

"I had heard of Emma Buck I had seen her. I was visiting an old woman as a charity case. This woman had a little baby—I suppose it was Doris. I understood at the time she was of bad character. I understood at the time that efforts were being made to put her in an institution, but I lost track of her. Mr. Dobbs came and reported that this girl was feeble-minded, though I have no personal knowledge of her having been sent to the Colony. I went to see Mrs. Dobbs. She told me this child was a good worker when watched, and that she had sent her to church and Sunday school and school until she could not trust her. She had left her for a few days on account of some illness the summer before, and she had left someone in charge of the child, but they didn't watch her closely enough. I saw Judge Shackleford and he told me that a commission should be held. It was held in his office, and the papers were sent off. They were returned because of some flaw, and they were sent to Mr. Richie, a lawyer in town. At that time Miss Wilhelm came, and the further steps were taken by her."

"Did you see Carrie at all," Strode asked.

"I saw her, but I never had any dealings with her. I never remember seeing her except that time."

"Your knowledge of the family began with knowledge of her mother?"

"Yes, sir."

"Who, as you say, was a woman wandering around with one baby?"

"Yes, sir. I heard she had had other children and they tried to take this one from her, but she yelled and cried so they gave it back."

"And in that way you were brought into connection with Emma's daughter, Carrie, who seemed to be following in her footsteps?"

"Yes. She didn't seem to be a bright girl."

"Do you know of her having been in any clinic in Charlottesville?"

"This girl?"

"Yes?"

"Not that I know of."

"Of either of them—Emma or Carrie?"

"Not that I remember."

Irving Whitehead signaled that there would be no cross-examination and Mary Duke stepped down.

8

The Trial: The Caretakers Speak

*H*aving introduced and embellished his portrait of the "defective" Buck family, Aubrey Strode was now ready to illustrate the merits of sterilization as a policy designed to be efficient and successful in reducing the cost of maintaining the mentally ill and "defectives" languishing in institutions.

With the testimonies of Dr. J. S. DeJarnette, the superintendent of the Western State Hospital at Staunton, and Dr. Priddy, the superintendent of the Virginia Colony, he hoped to prove his case.

Dr. DeJarnette took the stand first. Strode immediately established his expertise by bringing out Dr. De-Jarnette's thirty-six years of experience with mental defectives, as well as his familiarity with the new Virginia Sterilization Statute.

DeJarnette's agreement with the precepts of the Virginia law was readily apparent as he declared, "It is the best thing that can be done for them."

"For who?" Strode asked politely.

"For the patient and for society!"

Strode began to build his case brick by brick, "The first finding that the Board must find, and of course, that the Court must find, would be that the inmate is either insane, idiotic, imbecile or epileptic. They would first have to find that Carrie Buck is feeble-minded?"

"Yes, sir."

"Is the condition of feeblemindedness one that is judicially ascertainable?"

"Yes, sir."

"Are there well-recognized tests that may be applied that would safely classify those that are feeble-minded?"

"There are."

"What would you say was a feeble-minded person?"

"I would say a feeble-minded person was one who, on account of his mental condition, was unable to take care of himself properly."

"Mental condition in what way?"

"Any way that occurs from his birth or the failure to develop of his mind, would strictly come within the definition. Of course, insanity would cover the whole thing."

Strode's questions began to take the form of a learned discussion between two experts, "I understand that insanity may supervene upon a mind of normal development, but mental defectives . . .

"That is, feeble from birth," DeJarnette suggested.

"Now, feeblemindednesses is . . ." Strode led DeJarnette's testimony along the path.

"Is inherited and acquired," DeJarnette supplied.

"Is it curable?"

"No, sir."

"It is an incurable mental defect?"

"Yes, sir," DeJarnette emphasized.

"Therefore," Strode made his own conclusion, "it is judicially ascertainable whether or not any particular individual is feeble-minded, is it?"

"It is."

"In your experience, and in your studies, have you reached any conclusion as to whether or not there are certain laws of heredity which are ascertainable and which may be relied on in determining whether or not a feeble-minded patient is likely to be a potential parent of socially inadequate offspring?

"Yes, sir."

Strode leaned forward purposefully, "I will ask you to enlarge on that. I wish you would give the Court the benefit of some of your observations. Give them the family history, to a degree, of one of these feeble-minded patients—how far can you foresee of they will probably propagate?"

DeJarnette settled back, "Well, you find feeblemindedness runs in families. That is, if the parents are feeble-minded, you have every right to believe it is from inheritance. Occasionally a feeble-minded child may be from an injury, which will not affect its offspring—that is, it is accidental."

"Yes, sir, but if it is inherited?"

"If it is inherited, he is liable to transmit it, and I think Mendel's law covers it very well. Of course you are familiar with that."

DeJarnette began a long discourse on Mendel's Law and how it affected heredity and feeblemindedness, going on to illustrate this by a discussion of the infamous Kallikak family, who had more than one hundred defective offspring.

Finally, Strode began to weave in the case of Carrie Buck, "Now, taking the patient who, through insanity or feeblemindedness, is not capable of forming an intelligent judgment as to whether or not this operation would be for their own welfare, do you know of any better way of having a judicial ascertainment by the State as to whether or not it would be better to have this operation performed, then as set out in this act?"

DeJarnette replied, "I do not, and I would like to modify my statement as to patients being able to say what is good for themselves, because a good many are very, very anxious that this operation be done, to free them from the curse of reproduction.

Strode persisted, "I was asking you this question; if the patient has not the intelligence of mind to decide whether this operation should be performed, should not there be some tribunal somewhere to decide whether that operation should be performed?"

DeJarnette nodded, "It should, and this is the best I have ever seen."

Strode's voice deepened, "You have heard the evidence tending to show that this girl, Carrie Buck, is herself feeble-minded; that her mother is also an inmate of the same institution and is feeble-minded; and that Carrie has an illegitimate child, who, though only eight months old, does not appear to be normal. Taking these facts into consideration with the other evidence you have heard here in regard to her, what would you say as to whether or not she is the probable potential parent of socially inadequate offspring, by the laws of heredity?"

"I think so."

"You think her offspring would be probably affected?"

"I think so."

"You think she might be sterilized without detriment to her general health?"

"I do."

"Do you think her welfare and the welfare of society would be promoted by her sterilization?

"I do."

During cross-examination by Irving Whitehead, DeJarnette pointed to Carrie Buck.

"See that girl. She was a good worker and never brought into conflict with the law until she was pregnant. If she had remained sterile, in all probability she would have been there at home working with Mrs. Dobbs, who seems to be very fond of her."

Whitehead inquired, very politely, "Doctor, isn't it a fact that prostitution—that the bulk of the prostitutes—that the surveys show they are more or less feeble-minded?"

DeJarnette spoke in a firm voice, "I would say that

the bulk of them are feeble-minded. I am no expert on prostitutes; I am just giving you my general idea."

"I imagine you have a good many opportunities . . ."

"Oh, yes, a good many come there."

"Now, those prostitutes that come to your asylum, isn't it a fact that the majority of those are diseased women?

"What do you mean by that?" DeJarnette asked pointedly.

Whitehead went on, "I mean women with venereal disease."

"Yes, and one point I am glad you mentioned—they come there, having had children, and, brother, worse than all, white women come there having negro children."

"The point I am getting to is this," Whitehead's voice was firm and commanding, "take this girl here— let me state a hypothetical question—this girl is feeble-minded; this girl has an immoral tendency, as demonstrated by the fact that she has already had one illegitimate child. Now, if you sterilize her and turn her out on society, isn't it more than probable that with her having that immoral tendency and her sexual desires not being abated at all by this operation, isn't it more than likely that she will contact venereal disease?

DeJarnette answered gruffly, "Is it your idea that, feeling safe in sterilization, she will cohabit more promiscuously? Very likely."

Whitehead responded sharply, "Don't most of this type come under Dr. Drury's definition? They are fire-ships. They don't understand the use of preventatives, and therefore are more likely to contact disease. They are thrown into contact and have sexual intercourse with men who are normal men, and give them these diseases; say, syphilis? That man contacting syphilis ultimately gets married to a normal, sound woman. He passes on down to his descendents the syphilitic taint. How is society benefited by letting that girl out?"

DeJarnette rapped out his words like the crackle off a machine gun, "The man who will cohabit with a feeble-minded person would very likely cohabit anyhow and catch the syphilis, but the feeble-minded person is very easily over-sexed, and it makes but very little difference in my opinion she would be over-sexed anyhow, and that would be for only one generation."

Whitehead responded soberly, "But say this girl was sterilized and turned out, and in six months she had contracted syphilis, because, as you say, this sterilization has not abated her sexual desires at all. She does know she will not have any more babies, and she goes out and goes on a rampage . . ."

DeJarnette answered darkly, "She has already been on one."

"Well, say she goes on another."

"Very likely," DeJarnette murmured softly.

"So she is a potential distributor to otherwise sound men, and they get married. Now then, the offspring of those syphilic men come into the world with a syphilitic taint, how can you say that society would be benefited by turning this girl out?"

"Because I believe it would be just as bad one way as another," DeJarnette injected in a courtly manner.

"Suppose you kept her in that hospital all the time?" Whitehead said quietly.

121

"Well, you would not need to sterilize her then."

"Do you weigh her sexual gratification and liberty against her becoming, as Dr. Drury calls it, a fire-ship?"

"I do," DeJarnette said icily.

"And you say society would be benefited by turning her out?" Whitehead continued doggedly.

"Do you mean to segregate all of them?" DeJarnette barked.

There was an uneasy silence, then Whitehead went on, "I mean all those that are in the institution. Those women with the mentality of babies, and who, as you say, are over-sexed; who are likely to drift into the prostitute class."

DeJarnette's hawklike face was bleak, "And they would drift into it anyway."

"Not if you keep them in there. How does society benefit to turn them out?" Whitehead asked hastily.

DeJarnette's expression was thoughtful, "It benefits society by not taking care of them, and by the work they do. They are hewers of wood and drawers of water, and there is not very much more likelihood that they would spread venereal disease if sterilized, than if they were not. And then it is only for one generation, and the state is not able to pay for segregating them, and by having an in and out method, that is to take these feeble-minded, put them in for a month or two, sterilize them and turn them out; you can get most of them sterilized, whereas the state would keep all of them in."

Whitehead faced DeJarnette, raising his voice, "Therefore your idea is that the State Hospital, say it can only care for a hundred, takes one hundred and sterilizes them, and turns them out, and takes another hundred, and so forth?"

"Yes," the doctor said thoughtfully.

Whitehead settled in, "I agree with you that society would be benefited to that extent, but what I want to know is whether it would be well to take a chance on turning these girls out that they may drift into prostitution and street-walking and spreading diseases. Now, as I understand, in your institution two percent of the insanity is attributable to syphilis?"

DeJarnette nodded, "Yes. But what I am trying to say is, say you have one hundred in there now who are not distributing disease, and you have nineteen hundred out there distributing it and reproducing, whereas if these people were operated on and have a clearing house taking the others in and sterilizing them, you would have that many less reproducing."

"Now, doctor, one more question I want to ask you: This law here says that you shall not take sound organs out of the body. Do you consider the cutting of that fallopian tube. . . ."

"You don't take out a thing."

"You just cut it?"

"Yes, sir."

"Now that destroys it?"

"No, sir. It shunts the egg off from its destination where it would develop."

"It merely prevents reproduction?"

"Yes."

DeJarnette concluded and was permitted to step down.

123

Although DeJarnette's medical expertise was presented to the Amherst Circuit Court as scientific evidence of Carrie Buck's hereditary defectiveness, it was the presence and testimony of Arthur Estabrook, however, that was emphasized as scientific validation of the necessity of sterilizing Carrie and her kind. Aubrey Strode opened his direct examination of Estabrook with questions obviously intended to establish the scientific credibility of the evidence he was there to present:

Strode crossed forcefully to the witness stand. "Please state your name, age—if you don't mind—residence and occupation."

"Arthur H. Estabrook; age, thirty-nine. I am on the scientific staff of the Carnegie Institute of Washington, at Cold Spring Harbor, Long Island, New York, and my official residence is at Cold Spring.

Strode inquired politely, "What is the Carnegie Institute of Washington?"

"It is a private organization," Estabrook said earnestly, "conducting research along scientific lines. The department of genetics, with which I am connected, is a department studying heredity in humans, animals and plants.

"How long has this study in heredity in humans and animals been carried on at the Carnegie Institute," Strode asked.

"Since 1906 with respect to animals and plants, and since 1910 with respect to human beings."

Patiently, Strode built his portrait of Estabrook, "How long have you been engaged in this work?"

"Since 1910."

"I understand then that the work you have been

engaged in has been assisting the investigation leading to the formulation of the laws of heredity," Strode said calmly.

"This is right," Estabrook agreed, his thin voice rising.

"In those investigations, has there been any effort made to determine to what extent insanity and feeble-mindedness are transmissible by heredity?" Strode inquired.

"The studies on those subjects have been carried on for the past fifteen years, and definite laws have been found covering inheritance of feeblemindedness and certain types of insanity," Estabrook responded patiently.

"Have you yourself engaged in any particular studies tending to give you personal knowledge of such matters?" Strode spoke quietly, but intensely.

With firm dignity, Estabrook replied, "I have been studying those subjects since my connection with the Carnegie Institute, for fourteen years. The specific studies that I have carried out have been practically four: one a study of a large degenerate group in the northern end of New York State, a report of which is published, called *The Nam Family*. The second largest was the Jukes family of criminals, they being a family which lived in New York City, numbering about two thousand people at the present, whose record is of feeblemindedness. Four or five years I spent in studying the Tribe of Ishmael, situated mainly in Indiana and surrounding states further west. I have also made other special studies on other groups of mental defectives—that including feeblemindedness too."

Strode continued his laborious exploration, "Referring to this family of Jukes, when was the first published study made of that family, with reference to feeblemind-edness and criminality?"

After a short pause, Estabrook went on, "In 1875 a man named Richard L. Dudley (Dugdale), then officially connected with the New York Prison Association investigating the jails of New York City, found a large number of people who had been in the jail and later had a criminal record. A study made by Mr. Dudley (Dugdale) at that time showed a group of seven or eight hundred who were all either criminals or paupers, a few idiots; the term "feeble-minded" at that time not being in general use. In 1912 I went to the area where this group had lived and continued to study from 1875 until that time, finishing the work in 1915.

Wishing to nail down the particulars, Strode asked, "You dont mean you began the work in 1875?"

"No, I continued the study of them since that time."

"In other words, in 1912 you spent some three or four years in studying them."

"Yes."

Strode's voice had a touch of irritability, "Now, I wish you would say what was the result of that investigation?"

Estabrook said calmly, "Briefly, we found that the family was continuing to produce a group of mental and social defectives, and the result of the study was to show that certain definite laws of heredity were being shown by the family, in that the feeblemindedness was being inherited according to a direct rule and that feeblemind-edness was the basis of the antisocial conduct, showing up in the criminality and the pauperism."

126

Surely the error in the court record in Richard Dugdale's name must have been in the transcription and not in Estabrook's testimony. Dugdale had by this time become legendary among eugenicists. The revisit of his work with the Jukes by Estabrook and the Director of the Eugenics Record Office, biologist Charles Davenport, further elevated the fame of Dugdale and the Jukes. It also established Estabrook's and Davenport's reputations in the field of eugenics. Although they had earlier published the study of the Nam family referred to in the testimony, it was the name Jukes, along with Kallikak, that was to become synonymous with the concept of hereditary degeneracy.

Aubrey Strode's next line of questioning concerned the "laws" of heredity that had been discovered through the family studies that Estabrook had been engaged with in his career . . . Again it is obvious that he was attempting to bring the concreteness of science to bear on the question of compulsory sterilization.

Strode's voice had a cutting edge, "You say that the investigations of this bureau of eugenics at the Carnegie Institute of Washington has resulted in the ascertainment of certain laws of heredity, apparently governing the transmission of the attributes of human beings to their descendants. I wish you would very briefly explain to the Court just what the facts have been ascertained to be in that regard?"

Estabrook explained, "We find that in general characteristics or traits of the individual, either physical or mental, are inherited in pairs. A person has a characteristic or he does not have it, or he may have the opposite of it. As an example, a person may have six fingers. A normal exception to the condition of six fingers is the ordinary condition of five fingers. We know from observation, and have formulated the law that where we have the six-fingered condition, it is what is called the dominant characteristic; the normal condition of five fingers being the recessive characteristic. That is the dominant and recessive characteristics going together."

Wearily, Strode continued, "Doctor, we are not interested in fingers. I should have narrowed my question to what have you discovered as regards to feeble-mindedness.

"That reacts in the same respect to the normal, the feeble-minded being the recessive condition, the normal condition of mind being dominant," Estabrook said, patiently.

"What else have you ascertained to govern this?" Strode asked.

"Where feeblemindedness is found in two strains, the two strains meeting, feeble-mindedness will show up in one-fourth of the children. Where feeble-mindedness is found in one parent, that is, and only in the strain—that is, the other parent being normal but coming from a strain where there is feeble-mindedness, one half of the children will be feeble-minded. Where feeblemindedness is found in both parents, all the children will be feeble-minded. The rule, so far as we can find, has no exceptions. Two normal-appearing parents, both of whom come from defective strains, will in all probability have at least one-fourth of feeble-minded children. That gives the explanation of where the feeble-minded child comes from in families that are apparently normal. The blood is bad. They carry the defective germ plasm, and where two defectives' germ plasms meet, the effect again appears."

Strode spoke decisively, "I wish you would illustrate that a little—about the germ plasms. Take cases where you have a feeble-minded father and a feeble-minded mother, or a normal father and a feeble-minded mother, or a normal father and a normal mother, or what you call a feeble-minded strain in one of them, and show how your laws work out?"

Estabrook answered quietly, "Two feeble-minded parents will always have feeble-minded children. One hundred per cent of the children of two feeble-minded parents will be feeble-minded. Where one parent is feeble-minded and the other parent normal, we will have one-half the children feeble-minded,—if that parent comes from a defective strain. If, however, in this case the parent on one side—the normal parent, mated to a feeble-minded woman—if the normal parent comes from a good stock family where there is no mental deficiency; in the first generation none of the children will appear feeble-minded, but all of those children will carry a trait of feeblemindedness. If one of those children marries back into a good strain, the feeblemindedness will still be covered. It is a recessive characteristic, but if one of those children mates into a bad stock, irrespective of whether the mate is feeble-minded or not, if he marries into bad stock one-fourth to one-half of the children will be feeble-minded. In other words, it is a trait that is present in the germ plasm of the reproductive part of the individual that determines the offspring, and not the individual. We look upon individuals now as merely offshoots of the stock—the germ plasm is what goes through."

Strode continued, his handsome face bleak, "Now, you take the case of a feeble-minded man marrying a feeble-minded woman: you say all the children of such a mating will be feeble-minded? That is true?"

Estabrook's voice was still lowered, "Yes, sir."

Strode paused, as if considering the possibilities, "Suppose a feeble-minded woman marries a man who is not only normal, but has no feeble-minded strain at all?"

"I cited that case. None of the children will be feeble-minded. All of the children will appear normal, but all of those children will carry the possibility of having defective children, depending on whether or not they mate into poor stock.

"In other words," Strode sounded very pleased with himself, "they carry a strain from their mother which is likely to crop out in a succeeding generation if they marry another with the feeble-minded strain?"

"Yes, sir," Estabrook agreed.

"Suppose," Strode continued to probe deeper, "the mother is apparently normal but has a feeble-minded strain inherited from some ancestor, and the other parent is also apparently normal but has also inherited some feeble-minded strain from some other ancestor. What would be the likelihood of the offspring of those children—both apparently normal people . . ."

Estabrook interrupted him, "One-fourth would be feeble-minded."

"Can you illustrate this graphically?"

At this point, Estabrook began to illustrate his testimony by drawing diagrams on a chalkboard. Although his comments are somewhat difficult to follow, it is important that we see how those arguments are draped with the cloak of science. It is also important to recognize, however, that it is only a cloak. The existence of single recessive and dominant genes for intelligence is simply inaccurate. Although this simplistic portrayal of the inheritance of intelligence was compelling and popular, it has long since been abandoned by all but the most unsophisticated commentors on genetics. The idea was that the heredity of intelligence could be attributed to a single set of genes, called a "unit trait." This belief in 1924 gave enormous power to eugenic arguments for sterilization and the segregation of people judged to be mentally defective due to the transmission of the "bad seed."

Estabrook explained and illustrated slowly and carefully, "When characteristics such as feeblemindedness or insanity are present in individuals, we always put them in brackets. Here is a man who is normal mentally; he appears normal, but, according to Mr. Strode's idea, he comes from defective stock. Now we have the same supposition on the part of a female. Both of them are in brackets. Now, we know in the segregation of the germ cells we can show this under the microscope. We know the actual elements in the germ cell which carry heredity. We know those little chemical bodies—we know that they divide. Say that in the division of the sperm cell we know the character N goes in one cell and the character F goes into another cell. Now, if this cell, or nucleus with the character N, mates with this ovary cell, we have an individual who has chemical determinants of two normals. If this N cell mates with this F cell, we have an individual produced with the character indeterminate for N and a character F Feeblemindedness. Now, if this feeble-minded cell mates with this cell, we have another N-F. Now, if this cell here mates with this cell, we have a dose of feeblemindedness from each one of the parents. Now, according to our definition, and also according to fact, we find that those two people there have a character F, normal. These people L-K whose character F feeble-mindedness does not show, both appear normal. Now here is our individual. Feeblemindedness comes from that.

"Now, if you have two feeble-minded people mating, no matter which way your germ cells mate, you have nothing but feeblemindedness . . ."

Irving Whitehead interjected at this point, "What do you call a poor strain?"

Estabrook brushed him aside, "One in which feeble-mindedness is found by reason of birth, not by disease." He continued quickly, "Now going back, if this N mates with this N, we still get a poor strain, we get a normal individual, carrying feeblemindedness. Now if this person mates with a feeble-minded group, the feeblemindedness comes out again."

"Now," he concluded, "those are perfectly definite laws that have been found and formulated, and apparently the rule is not broken. I might add to the judge that insanity follows the same rule. Epilepsy follows the same rule, but we do not call it epilepsy, we call it neuropathic condition."

The court was then adjourned for lunch. When it reconvened, Aubrey Strode asked his expert witness on eugenics to move from the general principles of heredity

132

to the specifics of the case at hand. He asked Estabrook to describe his personal investigation of Carrie Buck and her ancestry. He also solicited Estabrook's assessment of the likelihood that Carrie would pass on negative traits to her descendants, saying, "I wish you would, please, in your own way, first as simply as you can, tell the Court what your investigations were and give the Court the benefit of the result."

Estabrook, in his own dry manner, spoke again, "I visited the Colony at Lynchburg, saw Carrie Buck personally, also her mother; made a brief study of the two; also read the two case histories. Then I went to Albermarle County where both Carrie and her mother formerly lived. I visited the home where Carrie stayed, also visited as many members of her family as possible. In this connection, I made a mental test of her half-sister, Doris Buck; gathered information concerning her half-brother, Roy, and gathered other information . . . concerning five or six members of the immediate family, mostly upon the mother's side. The evidence points to the fact that Emma Buck is a feeble-minded woman. That she has had three feeble-minded children by unknown fathers. The evidence further points, as gathered from my investigation in Albemarle County, that on the mother's side there are a sufficient number of cases of defective make-up, mentally, to lead me to conclude that the Dudley germ plasm, of which Emma Buck is a member, carries a defective strain in it. I have reason to assume that Emma Buck's father, Richard Harley [Harlow], was of a defective make-up, but not sufficiently so to include him in the classification of feeble-minded or that he would have been a custodial case, but feeble mentally. There are other cases to render the assumption reasonable that the Harley (Harlow) strain also carries feeblemindedness—that is, the germ plasm. That explains the reason that Emma, whose mother was no doubt normal mentally, and whose father was at least a border-line case within the classification of a feeble-minded stock, Emma Buck has three feeble-minded children, two of whom I have seen personally and the other one whom I consider so from my study of his school behavior and his general behavior reactions."

Strode asked, "Did you give Carrie Buck any mental tests to determine her mental capacity?"

"Yes, sir. I talked to Carrie sufficiently so that with the record of the mental examination—yes, I did. I gave a sufficient examination so that I consider her feeble-minded."

"Have you a definition of feeble-minded?"

"Yes, I have."

"What is it?" Strode inquired.

"A feeble-minded person is a person who is so weak mentally that he or she is unable to maintain himself or herself in the ordinary community at large."

Strode said calmly, "Now, what is a socially inadequate person?"

"That is anybody who by reason of any sort of defect or condition is unable to maintain themselves according to the accepted rules of society."

Strode's voice became stronger, "From what you know of Carrie Buck, would you say that by the laws of heredity she is a feeble-minded person and the probably potential parent of socially inadequate offspring likewise afflicted?"

134

"I would," Estabrook emphasized.

Strode's face was somber, "I read the definition of a feeble-minded person to you, taken from section 1075 of the Code of Virginia: 'The words *feeble-minded person* in this chapter shall be construed to mean any person with mental defectiveness from birth or from an early age so pronounced that he is incapable of caring for himself or managing his affairs, or of being taught to do so: and is unsafe and dangerous to himself and others, and to the community, and who consequently requires care, supervision and control for the protection and welfare of himself, others and the community, but who is not classable as an *insane person* as usually interpreted.' In your opinion, is Carrie Buck within that definition?" Strode said deliberately.

"She is."

Strode regarded Estabrook shrewdly, "Did you see Carrie Buck's child?"

"I did."

Now Strode's voice held a distinct coolness, "Were you able to form any judgment about that child?"

"I was."

"What is it?"

"I gave the child the regular mental test for a child of the age of six months, and, judging from her reactions . . . I decided she was below the average for a child of eight months of age."

Strode completed his direct examination of Estabrook with an open question to him asking for any further remarks that he judged important to make. Estabrook commented on the Kallikak family and the Jukes. In response Strode emphasized Estabrook's expertise by presenting a copy of his book on the Jukes to the Court.

Strode's face and voice were serious, "I hold in my hand a monograph entitled *The Jukes in 1915;* I wish you would say whether or not this book sets forth your investigation of that family?"

"It does," Estabrook answered proudly.

"It is, I believe, sometimes suggested that environment, rather than heredity, may be the prime cause of those that are termed feeble-minded. What have you to say about that?"

Estabrook fairly bristled, "The environment might react upon the individual in such a way that to the ordinary individual a person might appear feeble-minded in his actions, but the environment would not affect their inherent mental ability. In other words, the environment might affect the behavior of the individual, but would not affect—would not essentially change the individual."

At this point, Irving Whitehead began his cross examination of Arthur Estabrook. The fragility of his advocacy of Carrie's interests in the trial is again apparent. At several junctures in the course of Estabrook's responses to Whitehead's questions seemingly important and promising issues are simply dropped. This is true, for example, of both the issue of the difficulty of selecting just which persons should be sterilized and the question of whether sterilizing her would truly render Carrie more suitable for life outside the institution as was being argued.

"Doctor," Whitehead began, his voice pitched low and serious, "about this bad stock that we have talked about: those people were people with a feeble-minded taint in them—the ones you refer to as being bad stock. You say that of these children here, there are certain ones that are not feeble-minded, but carry the taint in them?"

"Yes, sir."

Whitehead reflected, "They themselves are not feeble-minded, but they carry the taint in them?"

"Yes, sir."

Whitehead smiled ruefully, "You, of course, do not advocate sterilizing those, do you?

Estabrook looked surprised, "I think not."

"The idea would be to sterilize them as the feeble-mindedness breaks out in the offspring? Sterilizing them as it appears (in them)?" Whitehead questioned.

"Yes," Estabrook answered with no expression.

"You have made a test of Carrie Buck . . . do you think she is capable of taking care of herself or being taught to do so?"

"I do not," Estabrook answered firmly.

"In what way will society be benefited by turning her out?"

"In two ways . . . you mean *after* sterilization?"

"Yes."

Estabrook began to lecture, "First . . . eliminating the possibility of her having feeble-minded children. And I might modify that statement by saying that experience tells us that the average feeble-minded person associates with feeble-minded consorts, so that the chances of her having feeble-minded children are much greater than of a normal person. Second . . . by obtaining her discharge from the institution. Her discharge from the institution would necessarily require some sort of supervision."

"You say she is incapable of being taught to care for herself?"

"She is," Estabrook answered sourly.

"And, therefore, incapable of managing her own affairs?

"Yes."

"And, therefore, unless somebody took her and looked after her, she would land in the poor-house?"

"No."

Whitehead was surprised at the response. After a brief, thoughtful pause, he asked, "Where would she land?"

Estabrook gloated, "She would probably land in the lower-class area in the neighborhood in which she lives."

"But you said she was incapable of taking care of herself."

Estabrook shrugged, "She is incapable of taking care of herself in the manner in which society expects her to."

"She is incapable of making the home for herself that a perfectly normal woman would?"

"She would earn a partial living."

"She would be a charge on the community?"

"Not under the plan of supervision of which I . . ."

Whitehead interrupted irritably, "I am not referring to that. You spoke of sterilizing her . . . suppose you sterilize her and turn her loose . . . somebody has to take care of her."

Estabrook spoke to Whitehead as if he were a school-boy, "There are grades in the ability to take care of one's self. I would say in the case of Carrie Buck she would not be capable of taking care of herself to the fullest extent."

Whitehead persisted, "Would she be able to earn a living?"

"She would be able to earn a living," Estabrook admitted, "a sufficient living in the proper kind of home where somebody would be looking after her."

There was a note of tiredness in Whitehead's voice, "The definition (of feeble-minded) says 'is incapable of caring for himself or managing his own affairs or being taught to do so.' This is the definition we are dealing with now?"

"Yes, sir," Estabrook agreed.

Whitehead elaborated on the quote, "And that he is unsafe and dangerous to himself and to the community?"

"Yes, sir."

"Well," Whitehead shrugged, "you would not turn a man loose that is dangerous to the community. Now this stature says society is going to be benefitted?"

"It will be benefitted," Estabrook's words had a honed edge of tension in them, "in that a feeble-minded person, sterilized, may, under wise supervision—to be perfectly specific, assuming that she be returned to the home from which she came, that of Mrs. Dobbs in Charlottesville, she would be able to maintain herself in a comparatively sufficient condition, from the standpoint of society."

Eyes around the room were fixed steadfastly on Whitehead as he listened to Estabrook's explanation. "So," he interrupted, "the idea . . . contemplates . . . that there be some sort of supervision . . . by someone?"

"Yes," Estabrook replied.

"That supervision would, of course, . . . look after their moral as well as their physical welfare."

"Yes," Estabrook replied again.

"So . . . your idea of the benefit she would personally receive would not be the benefit that Dr. DeJarnette particularly referred to?"

Estabrook looked confused, "To what benefit do you refer?

Whitehead lifted his eyebrows, "He said that . . . they might go out and enjoy sexual relations."

"She could enjoy sexual relations, assuming they were carried out under the sanction of society," Estabrook straightened his backbone, "that is, assuming that she was married."

Whitehead changed the subject, "You think . . . that she could not take care of herself. I thought there were certain grades of these people, called high-grade and low-grade morons. I thought they all came under the general classification of feeble-minded?"

"Yes," Estabrook's voice was strained.

"And that the high-grade morons were capable of being taught to maintain themselves to some extent?"

Estabrook realized where Whitehead was leading, "Yes, sir. If they are capable of being taught to maintain themselves . . . they would not come within the definition of the (sterilization) statute."

Irving Whitehead concluded his cross examination by questioning Estabrook on two other points which could have been of considerable benefit to Carrie had they been explored more vigorously and in greater depth. The first was the manner and appropriateness of Carrie's designation as feeble-minded. The second was the degree in which defectiveness as a genetic trait in Carrie's ancestors had been proven. With both issues, Whitehead simply introduced them and then withdrew, without question.

"You made a test of Emma Buck?" He asked politely.

"Yes, sir."

"You made the standard Binet test?"

"I made the short test," Estabrook replied.

"And, of course, you relied on the history?"

"Yes."

"You mean by that the commitment papers, and so forth?"

Estabrook disagreed, "No, I mean her history as she gave it to me."

"Her personal history as she gave it to you?" Whitehead seemed surprised.

"Yes, sir."

"You did that also with the girl here, Carrie?"

Although there exists no evidence that Estabrook ever met or examined Carrie, Estabrook insisted, "Yes, sir. Carrie gave me her personal history, which I also checked up in the field in Charlottesville."

Whitehead allowed the diagnosis of both Carrie and her mother as feeble-minded to stand on the basis of a short form of intelligence test and Estabrook's subjective assessment of their personal histories. This was the strongest scientific evidence introduced during the hearing. After a brief exchange on Carrie's ancestry, Estabrook's testimony came to an end.

Whitehead asked, "Emma Buck came of the Dudley family?"

"On the mother's side, yes," Estabrook supplied.

"And the Harlow family?"

"That is (also) Emma Buck's family."

"You say both of those strains have feebleminded-ness in them?"

"I do."

"And are socially inadequate—members of the same family?"

"Yes, sir," Estabrook stated, and was permitted to step down.

In order to comprehend Arthur Estabrook's testimony as an expert on the "science" of eugenics in a more personal context, it is important to know something of his life prior to and following the sterilization trial of Carrie Buck.

Estabrook was born in Leicester, Massachusetts in 1885. He received an undergraduate degree and a graduate degree from Clark University. It is interesting to note that Clark was the center of activity for the science of psychology in America at that time, under the leadership of G. Stanley Hall. Graduate degrees had been earned at Clark in psychology just a few years before Estabrook's time there by Lewis Terman, who became the dominant figure in intelligence testing in America; Arnold Gessell, famous for his developmental scales; and Henry Goddard, author of the Kallikak story. Estabrook, however, studied zoology at Clark and worked there also as a fellow and assistant in that department. From Clark, Estabrook went to Johns Hopkins University in Baltimore, earning his Ph.D. in biology in 1910. That same year he was hired as a field researcher for the Eugenics Record Office.

In a January 8th letter to Estabrook in 1911, Charles Davenport, Director of the Eugenic Record Office, outlined what was seemingly to be Estabrook's first major

assignment. He also offered advice to the novice field
researcher as to how to conduct his work and himself.

My dear Dr. Estabrook:

In confirmation of conversation, you are assigned to
the study of the 'Jukes' family, continuing Mr. Dugdale's studies down to the present and, as opportunity arises, checking over Mr. Dugdale's results and
filling out the gaps in the pedigree that he worked
out. For example, if it can be done conveniently,
continue the pedigree of Gretchie's bastard daughter and a mulatto.

The general plan that Dugdale followed is to be
used by you to give homogeneity to the study and to
permit of comparison of the later with the earlier
generations: but, in addition you are to pay more
attention to the analysis of mental characteristics
and the behavior of each person . . . Let your study
be directed toward obtaining a brief *biography* of
each person in the pedigree. Be not satisfied with
putting each person in some large class . . . But, for
you, each person is a class by himself. Instead of
'feeble-minded,' describe the mental limitations of
the individual. Instead of 'insane,' describe his behavior in so far as it was unusual; insist on further
details from the informant who uses such vague
words as 'not bright,' 'off,' 'bad,' etc., in describing
a person. 'Seek and ye shall find.'

I note there has been much mating with negro
blood. Seize the opportunity to make some study of
the inheritance of skin color, particularly the recur-

rence of black skinned children from white skinned offspring. We will send some color wheels so that you may express skin color quantitatively . . .

Finally, let me urge the desirability of being more discrete [sp.] than usual, on this assignment. The notoriety of the family is great; and you are so near the metropolis (New York City) that the chance is large that the cash value of news to the city papers is widely appreciated. A few innocent words to some 'bright' fellow in town may be followed by evidence of widespread interest in what you are doing such as may greatly interfere with our understanding. Be 'wise as a serpent and harmless as a dove.'

Sincerely yours,
Charles Davenport

There was to be a delay, however, in Estabrook's revisit of the Jukes. A year would elapse before he actually began that work. In the meantime, something brought the attention of he and Charles Davenport to another family. This family was to become known as the "Nams." They are the central figures in a family degeneracy study described in the book *The Nam Family: A Study In Cacogenics*, authored by Estabrook and Davenport. Cacogenics, another term used for the inheritance of negative traits through "bad genes," is illustrated in the book through the alleged transmission of alcoholism and "lack of ambition" through several generations of a rural New York family. Although there is no indication of how the "Nams " came to be found by Estabrook and

Davenport, it seems that the Jukes study was put on hold while the Nam study was conducted during 1911. In any case, it was not until January 1912 that Estabrook was on location to begin the Jukes research. Correspondence to Davenport from January through April of 1912 shows that Estabrook had found a place to stay in the community where the Jukes descendants lived, and had begun meeting knowledgeable and influential people who were willing to help him with his work. Although he was now involved in the Jukes study, all matters in regard to the publication of the Nam study were not put aside. Davenport and Estabrook were collaborators on the work and Estabrook wrote to his mentor immediately after receiving a copy of an advanced manuscript:

My dear Dr. Davenport,

I have received your manuscript and have read it over and have put in a list of corrections. A few minor ones I have put in the text itself. I return it by express. The paper is certainly fine. There is, however, one thing to be changed; my name should come first on the title page. When I came to you two years ago, we had a little talk in which you said that I would publish any research work I did, and it was with that in mind that I devoted myself most carefully to the (Nam) network. While the work in the field is most interesting, a field worker endures many snubs and unpleasant experiences. The thought, however, of the satisfaction of publication under my name has made the unpleasant part endurable.

Why should not my name be put first on the title page that I may have the credit of it. I have done all the research work in the paper, and, while you have put it in final shape, you will remember that I gave it to you unfinished at your request, that I might start on the Jukes during the winter.

When the paper is quoted, as it will be, the *first* author in the title gets all the credit as you well know. I am attempting to make a name, small tho it may be, in science, and I went into Eugenics with the advice of Prof. Jennings (a professor of biology at Johns Hopkins) and Prof. T. H. Morgan (at Columbia, formerly at Clark, and one of the prominent geneticists who became involved in eugenics) who told me that Eugenics was the field to start in now. Now, do you call it fair to me, in consequence of our agreement, to put my name second, and to take to yourself, who already has a worldwide fame, the credit of the *research* work which was done by me? Why should not the Record Office publish it . . . and give me *alone* all the credit for the Nam family. Scientific work is judged nowadays by its merits alone. I am perfectly willing to admit that I have worked for the Record Office solely for the credit of the research work I have done and expect to do now on the Jukes. With your name coming second, Mr. Rockefeller's demand that you stand behind it will be fulfilled. (John D. Rockefeller provided financial assistance for the work.)

I am convinced that I am right in the matter of demanding that my name come first on the title page of this epoch making work, for such it is or you would not put your name to it.

> Very truly yours,
> Arthur Estabrook

Davenport's reply on May 16th gives Estabrook a detailed discussion of how he had granted first authorship to students and colleagues in the past. He addressed directly Estabrook's concern:

> . . . in regard to your own publication, it was my hope that you would be able to prepare it so that I should be relieved of work upon it. After you had spent several months' work I realized that you were not in a position economically to spend more time upon it: that so far as I could see in any case the work would have to be overhauled. Going back to your raw material, I set to work upon it and spent three months of as hard work as I have put upon anything in my life and the consequence is that because of the confinement and of long night work, my resistance was so reduced as to render me quite incapable of work during the month of April . . . I should not have been able to do as much as I did in the time had it not been for the constant assistance of Mr. Blades of this office.
>
> When I got at work upon your material I soon realized that there was practically none of it which could be used in the shape in which you had it. It would not have been a credit to you nor to this office. The consequence is that, with the exception of two

or three pages descriptive of the first generation, none of the writing is yours tho based upon the raw material that you provided. In a rough way, it might not be unjust to compare our relations in this paper to that of a person who supplies a sculptor with a block of marble to the work of a sculptor who makes an image out of it.

As a consequence of all this, it seemed to me that, as the practically sole author upon material provided by you, I could not escape the responsibility of placing my name first upon the title page as the senior and actual author. At the same time, your name appears entirely coordinate as joint author in recognition of the research work, which you did, that provided the raw material for the memoir. I may state now that, had your work been presented in a fashion comparable to that in which the first memoir was presented (This is a reference to a study entitled *The Hill Folk: Report On A Rural Community of Hereditary Defectives* by Florence Danielson and Charles B. Davenport, which was originally published as *"Memoir No. 1, Eugenics Record Office*) or had it been presented so that it would not have been necessary for me to reconstruct it or rewrite it from the ground up, your name would have gone in first as Miss Danielson's did without a moment's question.

We look at the matter a little differently. You look for honor and fame in the position of the name, and I look only for responsibility. The publication of a work of this sort carries with it a heavy responsibility. It is subject to criticism. It has its limitations, and it is cowardly for one to withdraw from assuming the responsibility which properly belongs upon one . . .

I want you to consider this matter fully. At the same time, I want you to feel that the last thing I have in mind is to deprive any young worker of the credit that is justly his. If, after considering this matter fully, you still feel that the order in which I had the names on the title page is unjust, and that you wish to assume primary responsibility for the paper as it stands, I will very willingly change the order of the names upon the title page. But, in that case, it will be necessary, in order that the whole truth may be told, that a paragraph be added to the introduction, stating who is responsible for the actual writing of the memoir. Please present my regards to Mrs. Estabrook.

Sincerely yours,
Dr. Charles B. Davenport

When *The Nam Family* was published in August of 1912, the introduction to the study ended with the following statements:

The share taken by the joint authors in the preparation of this report is as follows: Dr. Estabrook furnished a description of each of the individuals considered, wrote most of Sections 2 and 19d, and arranged the larger charts. The smaller charts were prepared by Mr. W. F. Blades. Otherwise, responsibility for the books rests upon Dr. Davenport.

Acknowledgment is gratefully made of financial assistance from Mr. John D. Rockefeller in the publication of this work.

The title page of the work, however, lists Arthur H. Estabrook as the first author and Charles B. Davenport as the second. Arthur Estabrook had stuck to his guns and was beginning to establish a reputation for himself.

Over the next seventeen years, Estabrook and Davenport corresponded frequently. A recurring topic in their correspondence was finances. Estabrook frequently asked for more money in salary and travel allowances. Davenport often "scolded" him on the need to document more carefully his expenses and the allocation of his time. Estabrook was often in trouble with Davenport for taking unplanned side trips or otherwise engaging in activities not authorized by the Eugenics Record Office. Estabrook also seems to have had difficulty in using good judgment concerning the use of information he gathered under the auspices of the ERO. On November 22, 1913, Estabrook wrote to Harry Laughlin, who had apparently inquired on Davenport's behalf about a letter Estabrook had sent, while working on the Jukes study, to a state attorney concerning capital punishment and a feeble-minded man.

My dear Mr. Laughlin,

. . . On October 11, I sent the letter of which the enclosed is a copy to States Attorney Alling of New Haven Co. I supposed he would consider the letter confidential the same as the District Attorney here has considered confidential much information that I have given him. The letter was sent that a feeble-minded man should not be sent to the gallows. The States Attorney did not acknowledge the letter. He, either in court or elsewhere, gave out the partial contents of the letter. I should rather the matter drop entirely in respect to the newspapers. Shall I write to the States Attorney asking him why he did not keep the matter confidential? . . .

Sincerely yours,
Arthur Estabrook

A stern admonishment came from Davenport on December 29th. Not only did he lecture Estabrook for his having divulged information which should have been kept confidential, at least during the research, but he also expressed a philosophy which is seemingly incongruent with other policies and actions advocated by the Eugenics Record Office.

My dear Dr. Estabrook:

I have your letter of November 22nd to Mr. Laughlin about your correspondence with the State attorney concerning the murderer in Connecticut and his relation to the Jukes. It seems to me that it was not a wise thing to do. You should not feel free to give information to persons concerning others which is based on the data you are collecting. I myself feel that our data may eventually be used by the State, but any such use should be authorized by this Office. If this principle is not established, this Office is at the mercy of a large number of field workers, some of whom may bring it into serious trouble. I do not think the reason you suggest that the letter might save a feeble-minded man from the gallows is a good one. A man who kills is just as dangerous whether he is feeble-minded or not feeble-minded, and society has a perfect right to kill a person who is thus dangerous to society without any reference to his classification. The old idea that a person with complete mental equipment and moral control who should arise and commit a horrible murder might be hung; whereas another person without any capacity for moral control should not be hung seems to me to belong to a past age. It is safe to say that there are no persons who are morally and mentally controlled who murder, and, if they do, it is such a passing incident that it would seem far more reasonable for them not to be hung, than for a person without the elements of moral control.

. . . The general principle which I wish you to regard is that of not writing on the basis of the material collected about the Jukes. It is better not to say anything that is not absolutely necessary in order to acquire information.

> Yours truly,
> Charles Davenport

Davenport's position concerning capital punishment and the question of competence is that a person is to be held responsible for his or her actions without consideration of that person's mental or moral competence. Upon reflection, this seems to be an odd and inconsistent statement coming from someone who also believed that persons judged to be incompetent should be segregated from society by institutionalization, and who also advocated so strongly for involuntary sterilization. The arguments for institutionalization and sterilization hinged on the concept that persons found to be retarded did not have an inherent right to choose the responsibilities and privileges of citizenship and parenthood. These positions Davenport supported and advanced. In his letter to Estabrook, however, he argues that the same people who may have their rights taken away because they cannot act responsibly, should be held responsible for their actions before courts of law as all other citizens. A curious contradiction, but not of a sort unheard of in our own age.

The Jukes in 1915 was published by the Carnegie Institution of Washington in 1916. The sole author listed on the title page was Arthur H. Estabrook. He had made a "name" for himself in eugenics.

Estabrook's first involvement with Amherst County had come through his interest in a group of people of Indian heritage. Eugenicists had long been interested in the assumed negative effects of "race mixing." The Amherst Indian group was reported to be tri-racial, a mix of Indian, whites, and blacks. This, of course, would be tempting research subject for a eugenic researcher of Estabrook's ilk. As early as February 10, 1923, he wrote to Davenport reporting that he had begun to collect data on the group. On March 5th, Davenport wrote expressing approval of Estabrook's involvement in the Amherst research project.

Dear Mr. Estabrook:

I have just heard from Professor I. E. McDougle, who tells me that he expects to have all the field material ready by the first of May and would like to have you come to Sweet Briar for a few days to study the collected material and either write it up or go after more material. I think this would be a thoroly [sp.] warranted investment of your time. McDougle writes that he has twenty college majors doing field work and he hopes to finish it up in two or three weeks . . .

Sincerely,
Charles Davenport

The work did seem to progress quickly and efficiently. By August 4th Estabrook wrote Davenport:

. . . field work was carried out for a period of a month or so in Amherst County, Virginia, where an Indian/negro/white cross was studied in collaboration with the Sociology Department of Sweet Briar College, located near the area. The senior students in this department carried on field work under the immediate direction of Prof. I.E. McDougle of the department and my supervision. Approximately five hundred members of this Amherst group have been located, traced to a common head and studied; much illegitimacy and feeblemindedness have been found and a low social status present in practically all the huts and log cabins where these folks live. A complete report of the work will be made later . . .

154

Indeed, a detailed report of the research would be written! An indication of what was to come is contained in Estabrook's annual report for 1923–24 to the Eugenics Record Office.

> . . . The low mental level (of the group) is no doubt due to the preponderance of Indian and negro blood. The data gathered seems to show also that the stolid, unemotional make-up of the Indian, and so characteristic of him, dominates the light, easy-going, music loving, 'preaching' traits of the negro, for little music is found among these people, and no teachers or preachers have been produced from them, although there has been (a) school and church (there) for many years.

In 1926, two years after Estabrook's appearance at Carrie Buck's sterilization hearing, a book with the incredible and disturbing title *Mongrel Virginians* was published. It is the description of the eugenic study of the Amherst Indian group. The title page lists the authors as Arthur H. Estabrook and Ivan E. McDougle, in that order. It is the most blatantly racist of all of the eugenic family pedigree studies. It was hurtful to the people described in it, who had cooperated willingly when the researchers came with their questions. They felt that their poverty had been misrepresented in the book, and resented the distortion of their morals and habits it contained. Peter Houck, a Lynchburg pediatrician, reported in his book, *Indian Island*, that the people are still hurting sixty years after the publication of the racist tract. *Mongrel Virginians* was also used in the promotion of racially discriminatory and exclusive policies in Virginia and elsewhere. Although it did not have the clear national and international impact of *Buck v. Bell*, surely it rivals, in its own way, Carrie Buck's story as a low water mark in the eugenics movement.

During the years following the publication of *Mongrel Virginians*, Arthur Estabrook continued to do eugenic research and the results of his work were published as articles in eugenic periodicals. None of those works, however, garnered the attention that was given to his earlier publications. There are indications also that he began to have serious difficulties in his professional life and in personal relationships.

In November of 1928, Charles Davenport wrote to Estabrook's wife, responding to a letter of concern from her regarding her husband. After some words of comfort to her about some personal concerns she had shared with him, Davenport relayed an account of his own difficulties with her husband and his worries about him.

> In regard to the future, you realise [sp.] that I am only the agent of the institution. My every act is subject to approval and revision by the head of the institution. I know that the President has long doubted if I were wise in continuing Dr.E., certainly at the kind of work he has been doing. Also the Institution looks to me to see that the *greatest possible* return is secured from the money appropriated. I have had to make continuous defense of my plans of continuing Dr. E.
>
> Of late, I have begun to feel that I can no longer justify my recommendation that Dr. Estabrook be

continued. No replies come to my letters to him. He is on wholly unassigned and unauthorized trips. I have told him that the Institution will not permit me to pay his travel expenses, unless incurred on my order. I feel that the President would insist that the Institution should not pay his salary.

After full consideration of the matter, I have reached the conclusion that either I must inform the President that I can no longer conscientiously urge the Institution to continue his services; or else he must work where I can supervise his comings and goings, and vouch for his work. That is why, if he is to work in this department he has to make his home nearby.

After commenting again on some personal matters that she had raised, Davenport concluded his letter with statements that were less than encouraging for Estabrook's future with the Eugenics Record office.

. . . A man of Dr. E's achievement would have no trouble, I think, in getting a position in Philadelphia, in social work (Philadelphia was their home at the time).

Certainly the Institution would not approve it out of *Friendship* (if) I were to assign him to a place or a research, which would not, in my opinion, yield to the Institution the greatest scientific returns for money expended.

. . . I want to see Dr. E. very much, but don't know how to reach him. Please give me his best address.

Yours sincerely,

Charles Davenport

Within six months, Arthur Estabrook's ties to the Eugenics Record Office had been severed. Even his leaving was cluttered, however, by questions of his use of funds. There were several letters back and forth concerning a horse that he had acquired for eugenic research in the southern mountains, and then had loaned or sold to a friend.

My dear Mr. Davenport,

I am enclosing a check for $85, the amount of the money received from Mrs. Breckinridge for the sale of the horse. Her accompanying letter explains the reason for the delay in her answer. You understand, of course, that in the mountains a horse is sold with saddle, bridle and saddle blanket. At the time I left Leslie County, the highest I was offered for the horse was $25.

The camera is also being sent you by parcel post. I know of no other property of the Office in my possession.

I am sending you the final expense account. Your letter of February 25th seems to approve the expenditure of the funds on Feb. 23–25, a round trip to Philadelphia.

I am here in New York for some time now attempting to secure some sort of position which my particular training will fit in with. In applying for any position, it will be necessary to give references. Naturally you will be mentioned as my last employer. I shall appreciate a frank statement from you as to what recommendation you will give to anyone concerning me, when asked. Can I count upon a statement that I have done creditable work while connected with the Office? Will I have your complete cooperation in securing another position?

Sincerely,
Arthur Estabrook

According to *American Men of Science,* Arthur Estabrook conducted research work for the American Society for the Control of Cancer from 1929 through 1941. He was Assistant Executive Secretary of the Council of Social Agencies in Buffalo, New York from 1942 to 1943. From 1943 through 1948 he was Secretary of the Mental Hygiene and Public Health Division of Public Charities of Pennsylvania. In all these positions, however, he never again enjoyed the recognition and notoriety he experienced as a eugenic researcher. In a sense he lost the "name" he had made for himself.

Estabrook's role in Carrie Buck's story is a major one. He represents eugenics, not only the profession, but the self-interests of those who chose it as such. Other major figures in the saga of Carrie Buck's sterilization became involved in eugenics for secondary reasons.

Aubrey Strode was a social reformer who believed the plight of individuals and the condition of society could be markedly improved by progressive action. As we have already seen, he championed several causes which would have been considered quite liberal for his time and locale. He was thought of as a humanitarian by those who knew him well. He became acquainted with eugenic concepts through friendships, and his advocacy of sterilization was apparently based on his belief that it was genuinely "in the best interests" of the individuals involved and for society. Albert Priddy was a part of the political and medical establishments in Virginia. As a hospital administrator, the idea of eugenic sterilization probably came to him as a growing trend, an increasingly popular medical option among institutional professionals. He became an increasingly enthusiastic supporter of eugenics ideas. Ultimately, he was seemingly obsessed with the idea of eugenic sterilization, obsessed at least to the point of devoting much of his time to the passage and testing of a sterilization law.

Priddy was the last witness for the prosecution and had been the initial originator of the case. Throughout the preparation for and proceeding of the trial, he had been a very sick man, suffering greatly from Hodgkins disease.

Nevertheless, he was committed to realizing his goal of seeing the sterilization bill he had originally asked Strode to draft become accepted law through the test case of Carrie Buck. Despite his ill health, he kept abreast of each day of testimony. As the trial neared its conclusion, his health grew graver. On the day of his appearance, he walked slowly and painfully to the stand with the aid of a cane, his usual vitality missing.

But when he was asked his initial assessment of Carrie Buck and her selection for sterilization, he vigorously declared: "I arrived at the conclusion that she was a highly proper case for the benefit of the Sterilization Act, by a study of her family history; personal examination of Carrie Buck, and subsequent observation since admission to the hospital covering the whole fields of inquiry connected with the feeble-minded. . . . She was eighteen years old on the second of last July, and, according to the natural expectancy, if the purposes of the act chartering this institution are to be observed and carried out, that is to keep her under custody during her period of child-bearing, she would have some thirty years (still) of strict custody and care, under which she would receive only her board and clothes; would be denied all the blessings of outdoor life and liberty, and (be) a burden on the State of Virginia of about $200.00 a year for thirty years."

When asked to give indication that Carrie Buck was indeed feeble-minded and "the probable parent of socially inadequate offspring likewise afflicted," Priddy explained.

"In the first place she has a feeble-minded mother, a patient in the Colony under my care, who is of lower mental grade than she."

Priddy was Strode's favorite witness. He was very careful to have all the right answers. Strode had merely to provide the paths, "What is her name?"

"Emma Buck."

"She is also a patient in your Colony?"

"Yes, sir," Priddy grasped at the string, "She has a mental age of about seven years and eleven months, according to tests put up at that institution, and Carrie has by history and mental examination and observation, proven to be feeble-minded herself. There are two direct

161

generations of feeble-minded, and besides, while I don't know anything about their kinship, under my care and observation I have got about eight Bucks and Harlowes, all coming from the Albemarle stock. I won't vouch for their relationship—I don't suppose they know. I have one from Rockbridge County just committed; four from Charlottesville or Albemarle; one from Richmond; one at the Reformatory, and the other in Goochland County."

Strode sounded amazed, "They all trace back to . . ."

Priddy beat him to it, "They all trace back to the Albemarle Harlowes and Bucks."

"I will ask you again, what leads you to believe that Carrie Buck, if she had children, would be the parent of defective offspring?"

Priddy supplied the answer, "In the generally accepted theory of the laws of heredity."

"What is her age mentally?"

"Mentally it is nine years—a middle-grade moron . . ."

"Might she be sexually sterilized without detriment to her general health?"

"Absolutely she could," Priddy was an expert. He had been doing the operation for some time.

"Would you think her welfare would be promoted by such sterilization?"

"I certainly do."

"Why? And how?"

Priddy drew himself up, enjoying his moment in the sun, "Well, every human being craves liberty; she would get that, under supervision. She would not have a feeling of dependence; she would be earning her own livelihood, and would get some pleasure out of life, which would be denied her in having to spend her life in custodial care in an institution."

"Would you think the public welfare would be promoted by her sterilization?"

"Unquestionably. You mean society in its full scope?"

"Yes, sir."

Priddy dove in, "Well, in the first place, she would cease to be a charge on society if sterilized. It would remove one potential source of the incalculable number of descendents who would be feeble-minded. She would contribute to the raising of the general mental average and standard."

Strode wanted to establish Priddy's credentials, "Well, taking into consideration the years of experience you have had in dealing with the socially inadequate, and more particularly with the feeble-minded, what, in your judgment, would be the general effect, both upon patients and upon society at large, by the operation of this law."

There was pity in Priddy's eyes, "It would be a blessing."

"Of course," Strode went on, "these people, being of limited intelligence, lack full judgment of what is best for them, but, generally, so far as patients are concerned, do they object to this operation or not?"

"They clamor for it."

Strode seemed taken aback, "Why?"

"Because they know that it means the enjoyment of life and the peaceful pursuance of happiness, as they view it, on the outside of institution walls. Also they have the opportunity of marrying men of their mental levels and making good wives in many cases."

Later, when asked by Irving Whitehead about Carrie's feeblemindedness, Priddy classified her as a middle-grade moron.

Whitehead was again curious, "Is she capable of being taught to take care of herself?"

Priddy sighed as if tired. The question had, indeed, been done to death, "Yes, she is capable of being taught to earn her own living, under proper supervision. She is capable of going back to the home from which she came."

Whitehead took the offensive, "Isn't it a fact, doctor, that by sterilizing them it does tame them down?"

Priddy perked up, "It is not supposed to in any way interfere with their sexual passions, but I don't know. It seems to make them better."

"Doctor DeJarnette seemed to think it did not have any effect at all?"

Priddy got defensive, "There are no organs removed, and no internal secretions, but they seem to get on better. I don't know the reason."

"This operation, I understand, in a girl is just cutting that fallopian tube and tying it back?"

"Yes, sir. That is all."

"None of the ovaries are taken out?"

"No, indeed, that is criminal," Priddy was an expert on *that* subject.

"Now, most of those girls that were sterilized and went out and got married, most of them were diseased?"

Suddenly all of Priddy's frailty showed, "Yes, sir."

"They were of the high-grade type?"

"Yes, sir."

Continuing, Priddy gave examples of people at the Colony who had been sterilized for medical reasons and who had been placed successfully outside the institution. In an aside, he indicated that Mr. Whitehead himself knew the "inmates" he was talking about.

Mr. Whitehead acknowledged quickly that he did know these people. He seemed to want to clarify why he knew them and told the court reporter, "Put in there that I knew them (only) through being a member of the Special Board of Directors." He continued with his cross-examination, "Doctor, I understand you to say that if this girl could be sterilized, the Dobbs' home would be open to her?"

Priddy declared, "I understand they want her back."

"And the only thing to prevent her having an independent home is her child-bearing capacity?"

"Yes," Priddy confirmed, "the Dobbs' home would be open to her to return."

With this point made, Priddy was dismissed, and Strode began to read into the record the deposition of Harry H. Laughlin of the Eugenics Record Office.

9

The Trial: Expert Testimony

*E*ugenicists at the Eugenics Record Office on Long Island were the most enthusiastic advocates of human sterilization. They lectured and wrote voluminously in favor of sterilization on the basis of the hereditary research that had been done by their office and by other eugenicists.

The most zealous of these supporters of compulsory sterilization was Harry H. Laughlin. Brought to the Eugenics Record Office by Charles Davenport, the founder, in 1917, Laughlin soon became deeply committed to the movement to pass state laws requiring sterilization of people judged to be hereditary defectives. In this category, he came to include tramps, beggars, alcoholics, criminals, the feeble-minded, the insane, epileptics, the physically deformed, the blind and the deaf.

It is interesting to note that it was later learned that Laughlin himself was an epileptic.

Laughlin developed a model for sterilization laws that he presented to state, as well as foreign, governments. In developing this model, he hoped to influence "law-makers who had to decide upon matters of policy to be worked out in legislation regulating eugenical sterilization; . . . judges of the courts upon whom, in most states having sterilization statues, devolves the duty of deciding upon the constitutionality of new statues, and of determining cacogenic (genetically defective) individuals and of ordering their sexual sterilization; . . . administrative officers who represent the state in locating, and in eugenically analyzing persons alleged to be cacogenic, and who are responsible for carrying out the orders of the courts; . . . individual citizens who, in the exercise of their civic rights and duties, desire to take the initiative in reporting for official determination and action, specific cases of obvious family degeneracy."

Laughlin obviously had broad goals for his work on behalf of compulsory sterilization. In addition to his aim of influencing public officials and professionals, he hoped to enlist ordinary citizens in advancing the cause of sterilization by reporting their neighbors.

In June 1936, Heidelberg University held a celebration commemorating its 550th anniversary. Honorary degrees were awarded to a number of European and American scholars. Harry Laughlin was one of those so honored. The degree was conferred in appreciation of his services to the science of eugenics and his efforts to purify "the human seed stock." Laughlin's invitation from the dean of the Heidelberg faculty of medicine reads:

> The Faculty of Medicine of the University of Heidelberg intends to confer upon you the degree of Doctor of Medicine h.c. (honoris causa) on the occasion of the 550th year Jubilee (27th to 30th of June, 1936). I should be grateful to you if you would inform me whether you are ready to accept the honorary doctor's degree and, if so, whether you would be able to come to Heidelberg to attend the ceremony of honorary promotion and to personally receive your diploma.

Laughlin responded with dispatch and enthusiasm:

> I stand ready to accept this very high honor. Its bestowal will give me particular gratification, coming as it will from a university deep rooted in the life history of the German people. . . . To me this honor will be doubly valued because it will come from a nation which for many centuries nurtured the human seed-stock which later founded my own country and thus gave basic character to our present lives and institutions.

After the degree was awarded, Laughlin again wrote to the dean expressing his deep appreciation for the honor.

I consider the conferring of this high degree upon me not only as a personal honor, but also as evidence of a common understanding of German and American scientists of the nature of eugenics as research and the practical application of those fundamental biological and social principles which determine the racial endowments and the racial health—physical, mental and spiritual—of future generations.

Sometime later, Laughlin was discovered to suffer from epilepsy. According to his own eugenic theories, he himself might have been sterilized or kept in a segregated facility, such as the Virginia Colony for Epileptics and the Feebleminded.

In the report Laughlin submitted to the Amherst Circuit Court, he had analyzed information on Carrie and her family, and he offered it in support of Virginia's sterilization law.

The deposition had been taken in Long Island, New York on November 6, 1924, twelve days before the trial began.

Although there is no evidence that Laughlin had ever met Carrie Buck, he testified that Carrie was feebleminded as "evidence of failure of mental development, having a chronological age of 18 years, with a mental age of 9 years, according to Stanford Revision of Binet-Simon Test, and of social and economic inadequacy; has a record during her life of immorality, prostitution, and untruthfulness; has never been self-sustaining; has had one illegitimate child, now about six months old and supposed to be mental defective."

In commenting on Carrie Buck's heritage, Laughlin

said, "These people belong to the shiftless, ignorant, and worthless class of anti-social whites of the South . . . (they are an) ignorant and moving class of people, and it is impossible to get intelligent and satisfactory data."

On the physical appearance of Carrie, he said, "she is well-grown, has rather badly formed face, of sensual emotional reaction . . . is incapable of self-support and restraint, except under strict supervision."

All of Laughlin's facts about Carrie had been gleaned from Dr. Priddy. As to whether Carrie's children would be assets or debits to the future population of the State, Laughlin fervently declared, "The family history record and the individual case histories . . . demonstrate the hereditary nature of the feeblemindedness and moral delinquency described in Carrie Buck. She is, therefore, a potential parent of socially inadequate or defective offspring."

In point of fact, little was known about Carrie's child until much later. In a revealing article in *Natural History*, Stephen Jay Gould explained that Carrie's child was a girl named Vivian, who continued to live with the Dobb family throughout her brief life. She died at the age of eight from complications of an infectious childhood disease. Before her death, Vivian attended public school for four terms, from September 1930 until May 1932. The records from her school indicate that she was a normal little girl and an average student. She progressed well in her academic subjects and consistently received high marks for "deportment." In the spring of 1931, she was on the honor roll of her school.

In 1942 a successor of Dr. Priddy's as Superintendent at the Colony replied to a letter from a professor of sociology at the University of Detroit. The professor had written asking for information about Carrie's daughter. The superintendent, D. L. Harrell, replied to the professor with information which directly contradicted what Strode, Priddy, Laughlin and others had claimed of Vivian Buck and on which the courts had acted. His comments were simple, direct, but profoundly revealing.

> According to our records, her (Carrie's) child died during the summer of 1932, as a result of measles. The child was living with a Mrs. Dobb in Charlottesville, Virginia. She was reported to have been very bright and had completed the second grade in school. Our records contained no evidence that the child was definitely feeble-minded.

Although Whitehead objected to Laughlin's deposition being made part of the court record, he was overruled.

All together, Strode called eleven witnesses who alleged the mental "defects" of Carrie, her mother and her child.

Irving Whitehead called none. He chose not to argue that there were contradictions in Carrie's commitment record, nor that the Virginia sterilization law violated the United State Constitution, nor that it deprived Carrie of due process or equal protection under the law.

Within weeks, Judge Gordon decided in favor of the State and ordered that Carrie Buck should be sterilized.

10

Final Appeals

Dr. Priddy died of Hodgkin's disease in January of 1925. He did not live long enough to hear the judge's decision. His position at the Colony was assumed by Dr. J. H. Bell, who was serving at the time of Priddy's death as his assistant.

In February, the judge issued his decision. Aubrey Strode wrote to Dr. Bell concerning that decision and the future of the case.

My dear Dr. Bell,

Judge Gordon delivered his decision this week in the court at Amherst in the case of . . . Buck vs. A. S.

Priddy, Superintendent, sustaining the validity of the Virginia sterilization law and affirming the order of the board in that case.

While I regret that Judge Gordon did not deliver a written opinion, nevertheless, of course, the result reached by him was satisfactory and, by the appeal which will now be pressed, the constitutionality of the statute will be further tested.

In view of the death of Dr. Priddy, it will be necessary to substitute someone in his place as a party to the suit, and it seems to me that the case should now be carried on in your name as acting superintendent in the place and stead of Dr. A. S. Priddy. Please advise me whether this course is agreeable to you so that I may feel authorized to have you so substituted . . . "

Bell responded by saying:

If you are of the opinion that this case should . . . be carried on in my name, it is agreeable with me as I am in entire sympathy with the effort being made to reach a final conclusion as to the legality of this sterilization procedure.

And so *Buck v. Priddy* became *Buck v. Bell*. A. S. Priddy's name would become obscure except to those few people who examined the case closely. *Buck vs. Bell* has been presented to generations of law students.

In June of 1925, Irving Whitehead submitted his petition to appeal Judge Gordon's verdict to the Virginia Court of Appeals. His petition was based on three points: first, that it allowed the state to deprive a citizen of the right to procreate without due process of law;

second, that the sterilization law violated the Fourteenth Amendment which demanded equal protection under the law for all by being restricted to institutionalized epileptics and feeble-minded persons; and, thirdly, that the Virginia law violated the Eighth Amendment by inflicting "cruel and unusual punishment."

Whitehead's final brief, however, did not argue the grounds outlined in his petition. Instead it focused solely on the question of due process. It also proclaimed that most of the trial's testimony was based on hearsay, and that, since Laughlin's testimony had been read into the record, Whitehead had had no opportunity to cross examine him. The brief was only five pages long, cited only one case as precedent, and concluded with the statement that, if the Virginia law was ruled constitutional, then "trials are a farce."

In contrast, Strode's brief was forty pages long. Within these pages Strode cited many precedents, all pertinent details about the case, and summed up the testimony of its expert witnesses. It was a tour de force which focused upon the state's power and right to enact legislation to protect the public health and safety. Strode ended by stating that no court should stand in the way of the "path of progress in the light of scientific advancement toward a better day, both for the afflicted and for society whose wards they are."

Justice John West wrote the opinion for the Virginia Court of Appeals. It agreed with Strode's arguments and affirmed the lower court's order for Carrie Buck's sterilization.

There was only one avenue of appeal left, and, as Aubrey Strode correctly foresaw when Priddy had initially raised the question of Carrie Buck's sterilization, it was based on the constitutional question that finally had to be settled before Carrie's sterilization could be carried out.

Whitehead filed the necessary papers asking the Supreme Court to consider the case of *Buck v. Bell*. In September of 1926, Strode filed a new brief as well.

Whitehead's main argument was that a person's "full bodily integrity" was guaranteed by the Fourteenth Amendment, which promised American citizens the rights of life, liberty and property. Further, he said prohibiting a person from having children was an intrusion on this right. Against Strode's strong argument that the state had to have police power to protect the public health and safety, Whitehead maintained that police power did not cover usurpation of personal liberties.

At the end of his eighteen-page brief, Whitehead declared that if the Virginia Statute was upheld, the "worse kind of tyranny" could occur and the state would assume a god-like position of human judgment, "Then the limits of the power of the state (which, in the end, is nothing more than the faction in control of the government) to rid itself of those citizens deemed undesirable . . . have not been set."

Strode vehemently disagreed and proceeded in his brief to uphold the concept of the rightful police power of the state and its right to enforce eugenic laws.

On the issue of public health Strode drew from his own recent experiences of the smallpox epidemic in Amherst, in which the town had supported a program of compulsory vaccination, as well as from legal precedent to plead the state's right to enforce and insure the health and safety of its citizens.

The case was heard in April of 1927. On May 2nd, Justice Oliver Wendell Holmes delivered the opinion of the Supreme court in *Buck v. Bell*.

The court found that Virginia's sterilization act satisfied both due process requirements and equal protection guarantees. Holmes argued that sterilization was not too great a sacrifice to ask of Carrie Buck, and that "three generations of imbeciles" were indeed "enough." Holmes' diagnostic classification may have been inaccurate (the term "moron" rather than "imbecile" would have more accurately depicted the claims being made about Carrie, her mother and her daughter), but he was clearly writing an opinion which reflected the majority decision of the Court. Justice Pierce Butler was the only dissenting judge of the nine members of the Court.

The majority opinion of the court held that Virginia's compulsory sterilization law was constitutional. Thus, the precedent was established which gave state governments the right to become arbiters of the reproductive practices of citizens who were deemed to be defective in some way. In delivering that decision, Justice Holmes said:

We have seen more than once that the public welfare may call upon the best citizens for their lives. It would be strange if it could not call upon those who already sap the strength of the state for their lesser sacrifices, often felt to be much by those concerned, in order to prevent our being swamped with incompetence. It is better for all the world, if instead of waiting to execute offspring for crime, or to let them starve for their imbecility, society can prevent those who are manifestly unfit from continuing their kind. The principle that sustains compulsory vaccination is broad enough to cover cutting the Fallopian tubes . . .

Holmes' opinion that "three generations of imbeciles" was enough followed Carrie the rest of her life. Yet, the outcome of the case gave Holmes great personal satisfaction. In May of 1927 he wrote to Lewis Einstein, "One decision that I wrote gave me pleasure, establishing the constitutionality of a law permitting the sterilization of imbeciles."

At the time, the decision of *Buck v. Bell* did not seem to generate much interest within the general public. The *New York Times* ran only a small article. The *Lynchburg News* gave the story front page, but surprisingly modest coverage considering the local figures and the circumstances involved. The only evidence of public reaction to the decision—contained in Carrie Buck's file at the Virginia Colony for Epileptics and Feeble-Minded—was a postcard, postmarked Madison Square Garden in New York City on May 4, 1927. It was addressed to J. H. Bell and reads, "May God protect Miss Carrie Buck from Feeble-Minded justice." The words "from Feeble-Minded justice" were scratched through and "from injustice" added.

The card was not signed.

11

The Sterilization of Carrie Buck

---

*T*he significance of the case may have been slow to be revealed in some quarters, but this was certainly not true in Carrie Buck's life.

On the morning of October 19, 1927, she was sterilized by Dr. Bell in the infirmary of the Virginia Colony for Epileptics and Feebleminded. Her medical record at the Central Virginia Training Center contains these notations concerning her sterilization.

> Patient sterilized this morning under authority of Act of Assembly . . . providing for the sterilization of

ILLUSTRATION 5: Halsey-Jennings Building at Central
Virginia Training Center, where the sterilization of Carrie and
Doris Buck took place.

mental defectives, and as ordered by the Board of Directors of this institution. She went to the operating room at 9:30 and returned at 10:30, recovered promptly from the anesthesia with no untoward after effects anticipated. One inch was removed from each Fallopian tube, the tubes litigated and the end cauterized by carbolic acid followed by alcohol, and the edges of the broad ligaments, brought together with continuous suture. Abdominal wound was united with layer sutures and the approximation of closure was good . . .

Nov. 3, 1927: Patient has had an uneventful recovery. No infection. Is allowed up today."

Carrie's sterilization was performed without notice. Her surgery, however, was to have international consequences. The precedent it set would influence social policy around the world and would change the lives of tens of thousands of people. Within ten years more than 27,000 compulsory sterilizations had been performed in the United States. Also within that decade, thirty state governments had passed sterilization laws, many of them based on Virginia's model. From the time of the *Buck v. Bell* decision and Carrie's sterilization, more than 4,000 people were sterilized at the State Colony, which is now known as the Central Virginia Training Center. The practice was continued there until 1972. A total of 8,000 people were sterilized involuntarily in Virginia during those years and more than 50,000 people nationally underwent the same procedure.

Ultimately, Carrie's sterilization and the overall American compulsory sterilization movement influenced the development of the race hygiene program in Nazi Germany. On July 14, 1933, the model sterilization act developed by Harry Laughlin, the same one used by Virginia, became law in Germany. On that day Adolf Hitler decreed that the Hereditary Health Law was in force. The law was intended to ensure that "less worthy" members of the Third Reich did not pass on their inferior genes. Hereditary health courts were established to decide which persons were to be sterilized. Each court was to consist of two doctors and one judge—all government appointed.

The German law was implemented swiftly and broadly. By the end of the first year that the law was in effect, according to S. J. Holmes, over 56,000 people in Germany had been found to be defective by the health courts and had been sterilized. Hitler's actions were applauded by American eugenicists. Sterilization proponent Paul Popenoe felt that the Germans were following a policy that was consistent with the thinking of eugenicists throughout the world. K. M. Ludmerer quotes an editorial statement from the *Eugenical News* that concluded:

> It is difficult to see how the new German Sterilization Law could, as some have suggested, be deflected from its purely eugenical purpose, and be made an 'instrument of tyranny' for the sterilization of non-Nordic races.

It would be many years before most American eugenicists would comprehend the connection between eugenics and the stark atrocities of the Nazi regime.

It has been estimated that between 1933 and 1945, two million people were deemed defective and sterilized in Germany. In testimony at the Nuremberg war trials, the Carrie Buck case was cited as the precedent for Nazi race hygiene and sterilization programs.

In 1935, the Nazi government passed the Nuremberg Laws. These laws were based on the continuing German research on "Rassenhygiene" (race hygiene). The laws banned interracial marriage between Germans and Jews and elaborated on the original sterilization act. The articles of the laws addressing the issue of interracial marriage are chilling in the extent to which they mirror the influence of the American eugenics movement.

In reflecting on the connection between the eugenic movement in America and the Nuremberg laws, it may be illuminating to consider Virginia's "Act to Preserve Racial Integrity," which was passed into law in 1924, the same year that Carrie Buck's sterilization case was initiated. The act was written and guided through the state legislature by W. A. Plecker. Plecker, a strong believer in eugenics, served for many years as the registrar of vital statistics for Virginia. He also worked closely with the Eugenics Record Office and was a member of several eugenics organizations. A. H. Estabrook, the same field worker from the Eugenics Record Office who collected information on Carrie Buck's family, called upon Plecker for assistance in another study he was doing of Amherst's racially mixed families. In his book, *Eugenics in Relation to the New Family*, Plecker quotes Estabrook:

> Dr. A. H. Estabrook in a recent study for the Carnegie Institute, of a mixed group in Virginia,

many of whom are so slightly negroid as to be able
to pass for white says: 'School studies and observations of some adults indicate the group as a whole
to be of poor mentality, much below the average . . .
on the basis of the army intelligence tests. There is
an early adolescence with low moral code, high
incidence of licentiousness and twenty-one percent
of illegitimacy in the group'.

"The Virginia Act to Preserve Racial Integrity
states in part:

"It shall hereafter, be unlawful for any white person in this state to marry any save a white person,
or a person with no other admixture of blood than
white and American Indian. For the purpose of this
act, the term 'white person' shall apply only to the
person who has no trace whatsoever of any blood
other than Caucasian; but persons who have one-
sixteenth or less of the blood of the American Indian
and have no other non-Caucasian blood should be
deemed to be white persons. All laws heretofore
passed and now in effect regarding the intermarriage of white and colored persons shall apply to
marriages prohibited by this act.

12

Carrie: the Parole

*I*n Albert Priddy's testimony before the Amherst County
Circuit Court he was questioned by Aubrey Strode concerning plans for Carrie after her sterilization. Priddy
indicated that sterilization would allow Carrie to return
to her adoptive home in Charlottesville. This statement,
like much of the testimony in the case, proved to be
inaccurate. Although it is possible that Mrs. Dobbs had
indicated to Priddy her willingness to take Carrie back
after she was sterilized, no evidence supports the asser-
tion that such an agreement was made. Mrs. Dobbs'
remarks to Dr. Bell later, in 1928, certainly do not sug-

gest that she was expecting to take Carrie back. It is also obvious that by that time Mrs. Dobbs had come to think of Carrie's child as being her own and that she wanted to avoid contact between the two of them.

A few months after Carrie was sterilized, Dr. Bell wrote to Mrs. Dobbs informing her that Carrie was available for "parole":

Dear Madam:

Carrie Buck, who formerly lived with you, has now been sterilized under the Virginia Act of 1924, so that she cannot bear any more children. She is quite well behaved and a good worker, as you know, if a reasonable amount of control is exercised over her. Thinking that you might like to have her back with you, I am writing to advise that I will be glad to place her on parole.

Very truly yours,
J. H. Bell, M.D.

When Mrs. Dobbs responded almost a month later, she made clear her reasons for not wanting to take Carrie back into her home. Contrary to Dr. Priddy's statement in the Circuit Court, Mrs. Dobbs had anticipated that Carrie would be institutionalized for life:

Dr. Bell

Dear Sir,

I am writing you in answer to yours in regard to Carrie Buck. I am sorry to say that my husband wont [sp.] agree for me to take her back as we have the baby taking care of it and I don't think it would be wise for me to have both together. I think a great deal of Carrie but Mr. Dobbs says he can't take care of her as he is now in his seventieth year. Can't you still keep her at the Colony. If you would I sure would appreciate it so she would have a place to call home and not be from one place to another. I thought when the Red Cross sent her their [sp.] it would be a home for her as long as she lived and if you will keep her I would like to hear from you again. Thanking you."

Dr. Bell's final correspondence with Mrs. Dobbs did not give her the reassurance that she was seeking that Carrie would be kept at the Colony for the rest of her life. Instead, he explained that, in keeping with the philosophy of sterilization and parole, she would be kept at the institution only until another home could be found. He added that he was sorry that Carrie could not be taken into the Dobbs' home for "she was very anxious to go to you and she is a good worker."

In fact, less than a month after she was sterilized Carrie *had* already been paroled to a "good home". Carrie was apparently the first of many young women who were sterilized and placed in homes as domestic servants. Dr. Bell selected families he or other employees of the Colony felt would be suitable, asked that they send rail fare for the young woman, and required that they pay the woman a minimal salary.

Carrie was placed on a train for East Radford, Virginia on November 12, 1927. Early reports from the family with which she was placed, the Coleman family, were favorable. A letter arranging for her to visit with her mother during the Christmas holidays gave no hint of any difficulties in her new home.

> I am glad to report that Carrie Buck is getting on all right and say she is feeling fine.
> We expect to go to my mother's for a visit Xmas and she has a housefull [sp.] when we all get there, so we offered Carrie a trip to see her mother if it is satisfactory with you. Of course, we expect to pay her board or whatever the charges are . . .

However, in early January, the seeds of discontent had been planted. Mrs. Coleman spoke of Carrie in a different tone. The "chamber pot incident" it describes is a good example of how in the minds of many people feeblemindedness was equated with social mischief. The letter was written by Mrs. Coleman to a female employee of the Colony. She was likely the person who had recommended the placement of Carrie in the Coleman Home.

> Dear Mrs. Berry,
>
> We hope that you spent a pleasant Xmas and are feeling fine for the year's work.
> I dislike to have to bring my troubles to you and Dr. Bell but I feel the climax has come, when I went in the kitchen this morning and found Carrie Buck using the dishpan in which she had washed dishes, for a chamber. The picture I saw will never leave my mind. Of course I was furious, but was too tickled to

say much. I have written Dr. Bell asking him to take her back. I just couldn't stand any more of that.

I haven't seen Mrs. Brown recently but do want to tell her our troubles. I just want her to get a good laugh out of it and I'm sure she will. When you visit her we shall expect you to come to see us . . .

This was followed by a letter from Mr. Coleman:

Dr. J. H. Bell
Colony Va.

Dear Sir:

We are very sorry to have to relate our troubles to you, we had hoped to keep Carrie Buck for some time as she didn't mind work.

This morning my wife went in the kitchen and found Carrie using the dish pan, in which she had just washed dishes, for a chamber. She (my wife) said that was more than she could stand, so we are asking you to take her back.

We thank you for all past favors and beg to remain,

Yours very truly,
M. M. Coleman

p.s. Do we pay Carrie $5.00 a month as we did _____ _____ plus clothes?

On January 11, less than a week later, Carrie was on a train headed back to the Colony.

In February another letter requesting a servant girl from the Colony was sent to Dr. Bell.

Mr. A. T. Newberry was "anxious to get a good girl from your institution." He also described his family size ["my mother, my wife, and I, and two sons, one 17, one 7 yrs"]. He offered to make arrangements for transportation. An accompanying letter of recommendation portrayed Mr. Newberry as a "good citizen and a man of good charities and has a real find [sp.] wife. I recommend them for a home for any girl."

The A. T. Newberry family lived in Bland, Virginia, a rural and mountainous area near the West Virginia border. The family traces its roots in Bland back to the eighteenth century. Theirs is still a respected name in that mountain community where Carrie was sent to live in 1928. A. T. Newberry prospered and established a reputation for raising purebred cattle stock. This tradition has continued. In the summer of 1987 A. T. Newberry, Jr. was preparing for a vacation and the modern equivalent of a "cattle drive."

The town of Bland, which is the seat of Bland County, has the sepia appearance and character of a village of fifty years ago. It looks and feels small and manageable. Ronald Hall, the present Clerk of the Circuit Court, indicated that Bland is a town where everyone knows everyone. The entire telephone listing for the county and town consists of three pages. It was the nature of this small community, the connectedness of its people, which offered Carrie Buck a chance for a new life when she went there in February 1928.

Dr. Bell replied to Mr. Newberry's request.

. . . If you send me transportation, I will send you a girl by the name of Carrie Buck, who has been in the institution for years. She is strong and healthy and capable of doing good work. She is good tempered and easy to handle . . .

Mrs. Newbery sent the transportation money and Dr. Bell replied.

Feb 22, 1928

Mrs. A. T. Newberry
Route 1 Box 5
Bland, Virginia

Dear Madam,

I have your letter inclosing (sp.) check and transportation for Carrie Buck from here to Wytheville. She will leave here Saturday morning, February 25 at 7:20 A.M. and will arrive at Wytheville at 12:38 p.m.

Be sure to have someone meet this train and take charge of her, and put her on the right bus as she will be utterly lost if this is not done.

She is 22 years of age, strong and healthy and should render good services. It would be necessary to pay her about $5.00 a month in order to keep her.

Very truly yours,
J. H. Bell, Supt.

The day that Carrie arrived in Bland Mrs. Newberry wrote to Bell with news about her trip and settling in.

She explained that her husband had car trouble on the way to meet her train but that he had found Carrie waiting patiently for him at the station. She described Carrie as being willing to work and said she trusted that they would have no trouble with her. Mrs. Newberry then made a most telling query which reinforces other indications of Carrie's intellectual normality. Mrs. Newberry, after spending the afternoon with Carrie, questioned why she had been institutionalized.

> . . . Dr. for what reason was she taken to the State Colony? I ask this confidentially so if you don't care to tell me. We would like to know what to look for and guard against. If she is an epileptic is she apt to have them again?
>
> Please don't think me too insensitive.
>
> But I do want to know about her . . .

The answer that Bell gave is more confounding than clarifying. He said that Carrie was "not epileptic and was committed here on account of being feeble-minded". He added that there "is not anything special that I can tell you about her. She is easy to handle and not at all mean to anyone, and is perfectly harmless." The real answer as to why she was committed appears to be that she was poor, powerless and had had an illegitimate child. Mrs. Newberry probably would not have understood these as being reasons for being classified as feebleminded. At another level perhaps, Dr. Bell may not have understood either.

Carrie seems to have prospered in many ways while with the Newberrys.

Bland, Va
May 25, 1928

Dr. Bell,

Carrie Buck is getting on nicely does her work well, we like her very much, she is very obedient with Mrs. Newberry and I., but is rather inclined to be stubborn with Grandma (Mrs. Mamie Newberry) my husband's mother. She seems to think Grandma hasn't a right to advise her, but she has (since) this is her home. She often talks back to her, to correct her, and she takes it good humoredly. I believe she will do better now, this is the only fault we find so far.

She is strong, and so willing to work, doesn't seem at all lazy. She is expecting a letter from Mrs. Berry.

Very sincerely
Mrs. A. T. Newberry
Bland, Va.

Other letters from Mrs. Newberry consistently described her as a hard worker. She seems to have been genuinely liked by the family. Mrs. Newberry's later letter indicates a sensitivity for Carrie's need to have something of her own, a realization that eventually carried over to the importance of her having her own life. "Carrie seems well satisfied. I gave her some chickens and goslings to care for, for her own, so she is delighted."

In August of 1928, Carrie wrote Mrs. Berry to say that she had been trying without success to get in touch with Doris, but that her mother had written her a letter. Through these comments we become aware that neither mother or daughter was illiterate despite Oliver Wendell Holmes' comments that three generation of imbeciles was enough.

Dearest Mrs. Berry,

Will write to you this a.m. This leaves me real well and getting alone just fine. Mrs. Berry, I have wrote to Doris several times since I have been here and haven't gotten any answer from it.

I guess there are lots of girls going away now. I had a letter from Mother here several days ago and said for me to send her some things. Will it be o.k. for me to do so or not. Will you please let me know.

Give her my love and tell her I will write to her later as I haven't got time to write now as I have got some work to do.

Give Miss Viar my love and all of the girls. Well, I must close for now, with Love.

Carrie B.
Bland, Va.

That same month, Dr. Bell wrote Carrie, withholding a final discharge from the Colony for her for a while longer. Mrs. Newberry said that Carrie often asked about this. A discharge would constitute an end of all official ties to the Colony and Bell was apparently reluctant to grant Carrie such a complete release.

Dear Carrie,

I am glad to hear that you are getting along well, and giving Mrs. Newberry no trouble at all. Be obedient to them, and try to make yourself useful in the family, and I am sure they will be good to you. I do not think it advisable to discharge you, as you have no home of your own, and are not capable of looking after your own affairs at the present time. I will therefore, keep you on parole in order that you may have some place to come to in case you need help. I think, you should stay on parole at least a year before we think of discharging you . . ."

In early December Dr. Bell heard from Carrie again. She was clearly anticipating that he would be hearing some negative things from Mrs. Newberry. She was concerned about the effect this would have on her chances for a discharge. This and other letters from Carrie seem to clearly contradict, as does other evidence, the characterization of her as feebleminded, and illustrate that she was a literate and rational person

Dearest Dr. Bell,

I will write you a few lines to let you how I am getting along as I haven't wrote you since I have been away. I am getting along very well. I guess a lot of the girls have gone away since I have been up here.

Dr. Bell I am expecting Mrs. Newberry to write you about some trouble I have had but I hope you will not put it against me and have me to come back there as I am trying now to make a good record and get my discharge.

You have promised it to me in a years time but I guess the trouble I had will throw me back in getting it but I hope not. Give Mrs. Berry my love and best regards.

I have a real nice home and you don't know how much I appreciate it and they are just as good to me as can be.

Mrs. Newberry hasn't even scolded me about anything and neither has her husband.

We have had lots of cold weather up here. Guess I will close for this time.

> I am your sincerely
> Carrie Buck

The next day the letter that Carrie feared Dr. Bell would receive from Mrs. Newberry arrived in his office. Up to that point the only complaint that Mrs. Newberry had expressed was Carrie's inability to get along well with Mr. Newberry's elderly mother. This time, however, she spoke of a problem that was obviously very troubling to her. It was the same sort of matter that had caused trouble for Carrie before.

Dear Sir:

In regard to Carrie Buck I have never seen a better girl to work, and is as obedient with Mr. Newberry and myself as can be, and tries so hard to please us with her work and we like her very much. But she is beginning her adultery again, (I say again for I believe she is an old hand at the business). I feel that this has been her down fall before. I advise her as best I know and try to impress upon her the importance of living a clean pure life. She promises me she will conduct herself right, or try as best she can, as she hates the idea of going back to Lynchburg again.

So if she lives right we will give her a home as long as she wants it. But we cannot have this conduct in our home.

I feel so sorry for her to think that she cannot live a purer life. We have been nice to her. Treat her like one of the family. Have gotten her nice clothes, and has as good a room as we have in the house all her own . . .

But if she conducts herself right from now on she may stay on and on. She deeply grieved for fear of going back to the Colony.

She is also worried over getting her discharge. I don't know just how she would do if discharged. I fear tho that she will go to the bad.

We're very sorry this has happened as I had lots of confidence in her hoping she would make good. She does try it seems, but I guess it's hard to resist when once gone astray.

I must close. Will write later if there is any misconduct as I feel it my duty to let you know these things.

Dr. Bell replied to her letter, indicating his own perceptions of Carrie.

December 11, 1928

Dear Madam,

This will acknowledge receipt of your letter of December 9, enclosing a letter from Carrie Buck, the content of which have been noted. Her sexual delinquency is probably a thing that will have to be contended with for many years, unless she should find a suitable husband and marry and settle down: I doubt that she would find someone who would take proper care of her.

I am sure that you are doing your best for her and I hope that she appreciates it. This girl has a sister who was also delinquent: they come of a long line of mental defectives and delinquents, and due allowance must be made for the same.

Despite the venom of his remarks, Carrie herself continued to treat Bell in her usual gentle manner, and wrote:

Bland, Va.

Dear Sir,

Will write you just a few lines to let you hear from me. (At) the present time, we have a big snow up here now and it is still snowing.

I guess if nothing happens I will be at Lynchburg sometimes Wednesday. I would have wrote you sooner but I have been waiting to find out what time the trains run from Wytheville. It leaves there at 12 oclock but I do not know what time it is due at

Lynchburg. I guess you will know as you have met so many of the trains. So if nothing happens I will be there Wednesday.

Bertia says she couldn't come back there this time as she hadn't got her money to come back. I haven't been back there since I have been up here but I would love to see my mother. If it wasn't for her I wouldn't want to come back there. I'm sorry but it looks like I ought to think about her and come see her anyway.

Mrs. Berry wrote and told me to let her know if I was coming there for Christmas and you would have someone there to meet me. Well, I guess as it is bed time and I have to get up early, I guess I will close for this time.

With best wishes to you,

                                        Carrie

Dr. Bell responded with unusual warmth.

Dear Carrie,

This will acknowledge receipt of your letter of December 19th, and I am glad to hear from you. It will be all right for you to come down next Wednesday or any day it suits you during Christmas holidays. When you get to the station you can call up here and we will send someone to meet you. Let us know on what train you will probably arrive.

Your mother has been complaining a little, but is not seriously ill. Doris was discharged some time ago, and says she is going to be married.

> Very truly yours,
> J. H. Bell, M.D.
> Superintendent

Thereafter, the Newberry's perception of Carrie's conduct appears to have abruptly changed. A little over a month later Mr. Newberry wrote to Dr. Bell on another matter and added a postscript to his letter which indicated that a new kind of relationship was developing for Carrie. He also shows that he was concerned about the possible loss of her help in his home.

> P.S. Carrie is doing nicely now. Don't know for sure yet whether she will marry or not. But in case she does, please keep a good girl in reserve for me as I will want one.

13

Carrie: "I married Mr. Eagle."

M any social and political forces were influencing the nature of life in the United States and Europe during the years that Carrie was institutionalized, sterilized and paroled in Bland.

Women wore sleek dresses and garters. Couples danced to a new kind of music called Jazz. The Twenties "roared" financially and then collapsed into the greatest depression the country has ever experienced. Herbert Hoover presided over a nation that became frightened and discouraged. In Italy the Fascist program of Mussolini was being consolidated. The social climate in Ger-

ILLUSTRATION 6: Carrie Buck on the day of her wedding.
Carrie is in the middle in the back. Her husband, William
Eagle, is on her right; the Reverend Booze is on her left.
William Eagle's son and daughter-in-law are in the front.
Photograph courtesy of Mr. and Mrs. A. T. Newberry,
Bland, Virginia.

many was becoming ready for Adolph Hitler. Things
were brewing. In Bland County, Virginia, however, a
young woman was striving to secure the simple pleasures
of love and marriage.

On the 14th of May 1932 Carrie Elizabeth Buck
married William Davis Eagle. The ceremony was offici-
ated by the Reverend Raymond L. Booze of the Lutheran
Church in Bland. Carrie was twenty-six years old. William Eagle was a sixty-three-year-old widower. The marriage license lists his occupation as being a carpenter.

Three days later Carrie wrote to Dr. Bell:

Dear Dr. Bell,

Will write you just a few lines to let you hear from
me. This leaves me well and getting along just fine.

I am married and getting along alright so far. I
married Saturday about 11:30 and went to Ado, West
Va. had a real nice time. I married Mr. Eagle, a man
I had been going with for three years. I hope I will
get along alright. He is a good man. I thought it was
best for me to marry.

Tell my mother I will send her some things when
I can. . . . We are going to housekeeping before long.
I hope so anyway. I will be better satisfied. I will
close to a close friend with best wishes.

From Carrie Eagle
Bland, Va.

An acquaintance of Carrie's and William Eagle's,
Joe Compton, describes their life:

203

. . . I knew more about Mr. Eagle than I did about Mrs. Eagle because I knew him longer than her.

Sixty years ago the women did not travel as much as their husbands. They did not hold public office.

Mr. Eagle lived near the Court House at Bland. He served as Constable or Deputy Sheriff for some time before marrying Carrie.

He worked as a carpenter all over Bland County. Mr. Eagle was married to a Chandler lady before he married Carrie and [he] had a family.

The house he lived in is still standing.

William Eagle had been married the first time on November 10, 1891. His first wife was Nannie Chandler. He was working as a carpenter at the time and was twenty-three years old. She was fifteen. Within the next twenty years the Eagle family had grown large. There were four daughters and two sons.

In 1903 William Eagle was elected Justice of the Peace for the Seddon Magisterial District of Bland County. He was reelected to that office in 1907. During that same year he was appointed as Deputy Sheriff by the Circuit Court Judge.

In April of 1933, Carrie sent Dr. Bell news of her life as a married woman. Carrie and William had joined the Methodist Church in Bland, where Carrie sang in the choir, just as she had as a teenager in Charlottesville.

Dearest Dr. Bell,

Will answer your letter which I received yesterday, will send you a negative of my husband and myself.

When you finish with it, I would like for it to be sent back to me as it is the only one I have of him and myself. I am thinking about having it enlarged and some more taken from it to send my mother and Dorris (sp.), so please return it if possible.

I am getting along just fine.

My husband and I both joined the Methodist Church last Saturday and going to Sunday school and preaching both every Sunday unless we are both sick. We sure are having some windy weather here. We have made some garden, have onions and lettuce planted. We have cabbage, tomatoes and pepper seed planted and they are up and believe me, I will be glad when summer comes and I can caned [sp.] a few things to eat and have plenty. Tell mother when my garden comes in (I) will send her some things to eat and also a few clothes.

With best wishes to you and Mrs. Bell.

A Friend,
Carrie

Over the years, William Eagle held other responsible positions, including jailer, game warden, constable and town sergeant.

Many Bland residents have been told of or remember Carrie Buck. She was married in the Newberry house where the family of A. T. Newberry, Jr. now live. They still have the wedding picture of Carrie and W. D. Eagle.

Mrs. Andrew Kitts of Bland is a granddaughter of William Eagle. She remembers Carrie as a very pleasant

ILLUSTRATION 7: William and Carrie Eagle. Photograph
courtesy of Mr. & Mrs. A. T. Newberry, Bland, Virginia.

person. She has always wondered what happened to Carrie following her grandfather's death in 1941.

Mr. Edgar Dillow of St. Matthews Lutheran Church in Bland remembers Carrie and William Eagle in the late thirties and early forties as caretakers at the high school. He said that Carrie was a quiet woman but that she seemed to him to be a "mentally sound" person. He remarked sadly that he had the impression that she had been abused earlier in her life.

In August of 1933 Carrie again wrote to Dr. Bell. Her comments portray her affection for her mother, the responsibility she felt for her, the marital hardships being faced by Carrie's sister, Doris, and the realities of the Great Depression in rural Virginia.

Dear Dr. Bell,

Will take the greatest of pleasure in writing you just a few lines to let you hear from me. This leaves me very well and getting along just fine. I am still keeping house.

Dr. Bell I would just love to take my mother out for this winter and if nothing happens so I can't and if you will let her come I will make preparations for her to come and will meet her. I do not have but two rooms but still she is welcome to come and stay with me. We live out in the country. We have a pig and a nice garden and are putting up a lot of things this summer. I have planned on sending her a nice box but didn't have the money to send it with. My husband works regularly but can't get any money for what he does, it sure is hard to get hold of in Bland, but he is going away to work for a week or two and I guess he will have some then. The people who he works for furnishes us things to live on. We will send her the money to come on and will fix for her if you think she can make the trip alright. I am planning on sending her the money sometime in September or October, I don't know for sure when, but as soon as I can get it. He [William Eagle] has a daughter that is mighty bad off and don't expect her to live. I will see that my mother is well taken care of and plenty to eat if you will let her come. I am real anxious for her to come. I had a letter from Dorris [sp.] sometime ago and said that her husband had left her. I am sorry about that. (I) was hoping she would do well. She said she was going to get a divorce for her husband and for not taking care of her. She wrote for me to send her a pair of shoes and a dress but I didn't have any money to buy them. Well I guess I will close for it is bed time for me. Answer real soon.

> As ever. Yours truly,
> Mrs. W. D. Eagle

Carrie continued to care for and about her mother. By the end of August, she began formulating plans to have her mother live with her. But she was never able to implement the plan, due to her own strained finances and perhaps because of her "unstable" history as a former resident of the Colony for Epileptics and Feeble-minded.

Dear Carrie:

This will acknowledge receipt of your letter of August 19th enclosing one for your mother, which has been sent to her.

I am sorry you have been sick and hope you are all right again.

If you want to take your mother to live with you, and you can support her and take care of her, and it is agreeable to your husband, it will be all right with me. You had better think it over well, however, before you take any steps in the matter.

> Very truly yours,
> J. H. Bell, M.D.
> Superintendent

In October of 1940, she wrote to the new Superintendent of the Colony, Dr. Arnold, regarding her mother's welfare.

Dr. J. B. Arnold
Colony, Va

Dear Sir,

Will drop you a few lines in regards to my mother Emmett Buck. I have not heard from her for sometime. I would like to her [sp.] from her, and to find out how she is, and if she is well. So please if it is convenient and not to [sp.] much trouble please let me know at once how she is. I would like if she is still living, to send her a box. Thank you.

> With best regards,
> Mrs. Carrie Eagle
> Bland, Va.

And Dr. Arnold responded to her.

Mrs. Carrie Eagle
Bland, Virginia

Your mother, Mrs. Emma Buck, is still well and healthy. She is not quite as stout as she was at one time and is getting somewhat feeble, but is still able to get around on her own power pretty well.

She remains happy most of the time.

> Yours very truly,
> G. B. Arnold, M.d.
> Superintendent

These are the last letters in Carrie's file.

Two earlier letters, however, contain an amazing request from Dr. Bell and an equally amazing response from Carrie.

My dear Carrie:

A gentleman in California who is publishing a history of sterilization has asked me to get a picture of you to put in his book, as you were the first person sterilized under the Virginia law. If you can get this picture taken and send it to me, I will forward it to the gentleman who is interested in publishing this book. I should say that a Kodak picture of about post card size would be all right.

I would also like to get a picture of the infant born to you just before you came here, if you have one you could send me; or if you will tell me where the child is, I will endeavor to get a picture of it.

Please attend to this right away . . .

Carrie responded to Dr. Bell's request.

Dearest Dr. Bell,

In regards to your letter I received several days ago, will answer today. . . . I haven't got the picture in which you wrote me for, but I have a negative of my husband and myself taken together, if you can have one taken off of it and send it to the man in which you were telling me about in your letter, I will be glad to let you have it, so please answer right away and let me know about it and I will send it directly to you. I am getting just fine and am in good health. I have gone to house-keeping and like it just fine. Have been housekeeping now about 5 or six months. My husband and I both have joined church. We joined the Methodist church.

I have turned a new leaf and am trying to live to it now as I now [sp.] that if I don't do it I am lost in the world without anywhere to go, and so long as my husband lives I will be well taken care of.

We have a nice garden spot and tell my mother whenever I can do it I will send her some things. We are pretty hard up now for a good many thing but still we are thankful for what we have got in this world.

211

Will close for now. Give all the girls there my best wishes.

> With best wishes,
> Mrs. Carrie Eagle

Answer this real soon and let me know what to do about the picture. I do not know where you can get a picture of Babie.

Although she said that she did not know where Dr. Bell could get a picture of "Babie," Carrie later revealed to one of the authors, Ray Nelson, that she not only knew where Vivian was living, but had seen the child whom she described as "so very sweet."

14

Carrie: The Rest of Her Life

W̲illiam Eagle died in 1941. Not long afterward, Carrie moved to Front Royal, which lies in the northwest portion of Virginia near large apple orchards that employ agricultural workers. Late in her life Carrie told a social worker that one of her occupations had been "migrant worker."

A good friend of Carrie's, Lucille Lewis, revealed to Dr. Smith that her mother and father had been cared for by Carrie in their declining years. She had taken care of all their needs, keeping house for them and acting as their nurse. According to Mrs. Lewis, Carrie was a "nice, kind person." As to having been diagnosed as mentally retarded, Mrs. Lewis said that she did not believe that was ever true of Carrie. She said, "She knew what she was doing, there was nothing wrong with that woman's mind."

After Carrie was placed in a nursing home later in her life, Mrs. Lewis often sent her the Front Royal newspaper. She said, "Carrie watched for that paper—she lived to get that paper."

Before Lucille Lewis hired Carrie to take care of her parents, Carrie had "kept house" for another woman in Front Royal. Life had not been easy for Carrie during that time. When Carrie left her job, she weighed only 100 pounds. Carrie had been terribly overworked during this period. Later, Carrie was to suffer another serious health problem; she had a breast removed.

When Carrie's sister, Doris, died, Mrs. Lewis went to Carrie's nursing home in Waynesboro (a two-hour drive from Front Royal) and brought Carrie back for the funeral.

In May of 1987, Dr. Smith visited with Mrs. Lewis in her home in Front Royal. She recalled that she had first been aware of Carrie's being in Front Royal in the early fifties. She said that Carrie lived with a woman who had an "afflicted" grandson. She explained that the grandson was born "all twisted" and that Carrie took care of him. Carrie also cared for the grandmother who was herself elderly and ill. It was during this period that Carrie lost considerable weight and was apparently close to exhaustion. When the grandmother died and other arrangements were made for the grandson, Mrs. Lewis took Carrie to her home, "I took her home and nursed and fed

214

her for several months." Mrs. Lewis then gave Carrie the job of caring for her parents.

Mrs. Lewis said that Carrie never talked much about herself, but that she had washed dishes in a local restaurant at one time. She also remembers that Carrie was very close to her sister, Doris and continued to stay in touch with her brother Roy, who subsequently married and had three children: two girls and a boy.

On April 25, 1965, Carrie was married for the second time to a man named Charles Albert Detamore, who lived in Warren County where they were married. She was sixty-two years old at the time. He was sixty-one.

Charles Detamore was an orchard worker. Both he and Carrie had been born in Albemarle County, which surrounds the city of Charlottesville. Perhaps it was this commonality which helped to bring them together. They were married by J. Moreau, a Presbyterian minister.

In June of 1987, Lemuel Figgins, a brother-in-law of Carrie's sister Doris said he saw Carrie several times and heard her sister Doris speak of her often. He usually saw her at Doris' and Matt's home. Doris and Matt (Doris's second husband) were married in Charlottesville and then moved to Washington.

Lemuel was certain that Carrie was not retarded. He said she was "sharp." She had educated herself and worked at a restaurant in Front Royal at one time.

Carrie's health began to deteriorate in 1970, so she and her husband went back to Charlottesville. Their home was a single-room, cinder-block shed, with no plumbing. Unlike Dr. Bell's report that Carrie, after her sterilization, "was immediately returned to society and made good," she lived in abject poverty for the last ten years of her life.

During the 1970's, when one of the authors of this book, Dr. Nelson, was director of the institution now known as the Central Virginia Training Center, he conducted research on the Center's records relating to the practice of sterilization. He was interested in finding out what he could about Carrie and her sister Doris. Doris, as discussed earlier, had also been placed in the Colony and had been sterilized there. While reviewing the files, he discovered the fact that following the *Buck v. Bell* decision and Carrie's sterilization, literally thousands of people had been sterilized in that one institution.

In 1979, Dr. Nelson located Carrie and Doris. Doris and Matthew Figgins were still living in Front Royal. They had been married for 39 years. While visiting with them, Nelson brought out copies of institutional records that Doris was interested in knowing about. He read to her some of the important dates from the files, including her birth date, which she had not known. When he read the date of her sterilization, he heard a cry. Looking up from the records he was reading, he saw Doris and Matthew sobbing. In an article in the *Richmond Times Dispatch*, Nelson revealed,

"They didn't know she'd been sterilized."

Doris told him that when she was wheeled into an operating room at the Lynchburg hospital at the age of 16 in 1928, doctors indicated only that they were going to perform an appendectomy.

"Here was this lady," Dr. Nelson said, "who for

ILLUSTRATION 8: Charlie and Carrie Detamore. Photograph
courtesy of Mrs. Lucille Lewis, Front Royal, Virginia.

years had been feeling that she had failed because she couldn't have children."

Through Doris, Nelson was able to locate Carrie, who was living with her husband, Charlie Detamore, in Albemarle County.

In subsequent newspaper interviews with *The Daily Advance* of Lynchburg, Carrie told reporters that the operation was performed on her because she got pregnant and had a baby by a nephew of the Dobbs, who had raped her. She explained that she was told only that she had to have an operation, not that it would mean she could never have a child again. She said that she did not really understand that she had been sterilized until several years after the operation was performed. "I didn't want a big family," she said in an interview, but "I'd like to have a couple of children." She said, "I was surprised. Oh yea, I was angry . . . I just didn't like the idea of being operated on to keep from having children."

On July 4, 1980, Dr. Nelson decided, at Carrie's and Doris's urging, to take them back to the Colony, so that they might visit their mother's grave for the first time. Doris's husband drove.

There were tears in both daughters' eyes as they bent over the grave in the "Briar Patch" to pull up some of the dense growth of weeds and place a few blossoms near the simple stone marker.

Then they all slowly walked back to the building which had been the site of the infirmary where both women had been operated on without their consent. Carrie, grown old and fragile, her legs troubling her, could go no further and sat down to rest. Doris led Dr. Nelson upstairs to the room where the operation had taken place. With a touch of the defiant spirit, which was reminiscent of her mother, she pointed to the operating table which had altered her life on that ominous day in 1928 when she, like her sister before her, had been sterilized.

Paul Lombardo, in connection with his own exploration of *Buck v. Bell,* also visited Carrie during the last years of her life. In a letter to Stephen Jay Gould which was quoted in Gould's *Natural History* article, he remarked:

> As for Carrie, when I met her she was reading newspapers daily and joining a more literate friend to assist at regular bouts with the crossword puzzles. She was not a sophisticated woman, and lacked social graces, but mental health professionals who examined her in later life confirmed my impressions that she was neither mentally ill nor retarded.

Carrie died in 1983. At the time of her death she was living at the District Home in Waynesboro, Virginia. She had been brought there after she and her husband Charlie were discovered living in poverty near Charlottesville. They were first treated for malnutrition and exposure at the University of Virginia Hospital and then brought to Waynesboro.

In January of 1986 Mr. Jerry Layman, the Administrator of the District Home, wrote: "Thank you for your letter of January 7, 1986 requesting information on Carrie Detamore. Her husband, Charles Detamore, passed away here October 17, 1985." Dr. Smith later visited the District Home and talked with Mr. Layman and with the

ILLUSTRATION 9: Shortly before her death, Carrie portrayed
Mary in the nursing home's Christmas pageant. Photograph
courtesy of The District Home,
Waynesboro, Virginia.

Home's social worker, Sharon Kincaid. Ms. Kincaid described Carrie as an active resident of the Home, participating in reading groups and other recreational activities. She enjoyed music and dramatics. Ms. Kincaid had a strong memory of Carrie's devotion to her husband; Carrie often used her own canteen allotment to buy candy, cupcakes and cigarettes for Charlie. She was always thinking of his welfare, and some of the staff of the Home felt that she sacrificed too much for him.

Ms. Kincaid spoke with obvious affection for Carrie. She referred to her as an "alert and pleasant lady." She too, as so many who knew Carrie in her later life, rejected the notion that Carrie could have been mentally retarded.

Carrie is buried in Charlottesville in the same cemetery as her daughter Vivian. The cemetery, in an old section of the town, is surrounded by almost identical blocks of small, shingled houses, with their patches of green grass.

On a hot summer day in 1987, Dr. Smith drove through the winding streets, trying to locate the site. When he finally saw it, he got out of his car only to find that, from the street, the cemetery had seemed deceptively small. Indeed, the monuments and markers stretched on and on. Wearily trudging from one section to the next, he was about to give up when he spied a group of workers closing a fresh grave. Luckily, the chief caretaker was among them. He checked his records and quickly found Carrie's name. He did not have Vivian's name in the directory and, at first, had no idea of where to look. Then Dr. Smith realized that her burial would likely have been arranged by the Dobbs family. The caretaker immediately took Dr. Smith to the Dobbs' family plot.

There, in the shadows of a large family gravestone, was Vivian's simple marker.

Carrie and her child Vivian are buried a distance from each other, perhaps fifty yards. Their graves are on opposite hillsides. Between them lies a valley. A feeling of deep sadness comes as one walks there. A haunting image endures. In sight of each other, by all rights belonging to each other, this final barrier will separate them in death, as so many others did in life.

15

Carrie's Family: The Irony

*T*here is a great deal of interest in the United States today in genealogical research. For the last five years one of the authors, Dr. Smith, has been engaged in work that has taken him frequently to courthouses and historical societies. There are almost always people in these places searching for information on their own families. The National Archives has a large room equipped with microfilm readers. The room is literally filled each day by people searching for their own roots.

After studying family histories and some of the uses which have been made of family histories, he is convinced that it is possible to find whatever you wish to find in a family tree. If you are seeking your own tie to wealth or greatness, go back far enough and range widely enough with your investigation and you are bound to find it. If you are trying to find skeletons in someone else's closet, follow the same path—you will find them. It has been said that by the use of statistics any body of data may be variously manipulated so as to support opposing conclusions. The same is true of what might be called "genealogical manipultion." By examining a few generations of a family and their horizontal relations, widely differing tales may be told depending on whom you chose to talk about.

Because it is possible to find different stories in the same family, the eugenicists discovered that family history was a powerful tool with which to uncover material supportive of their hereditary claims. Deborah Kallikak, Carrie Buck and others were used, along with their families, to show how "they" are inferior to "us" and "we" are superior to "them." "They" were used to show the necessity for "us" controlling "them."

Alex Shoumatoff, in his book *The Mountain of Names*, points out that everyone is part of a huge pyramid of descendants coming down from the earliest human beings, and at the same time, each of us does have a separate family pedigree. These separate pedigrees, however, overlap at literally millions of junctures. It is amazing, when these junctures are examined, to discover the relationships which exist. Shoumatoff cites, for example, the work of genealogist William Addams Reitwiesner who discovered that:

... Hamilton Jordan, former President Jimmy Carter's top aide, and former Florida Governor Reuben Askew are eighth cousins once removed; that Carter and former President Richard Nixon are sixth cousins . . . ; that Nixon and Vice-President Bush are tenth cousins once removed; that Bush is a seventh cousin of Elliot Richardson, attorney general in the Nixon Administration, as well as being a kinsman of Ernest Hemingway and of the nineteenth century plutocrat Jay Gould; and that the California senator Alan Cranston has in his constellation of known kin, through common descent from a man named Robert Bullard, who lived in Watertown, Massachusetts in the early sixteen hundreds; Queen Geraldine of Albania, Richard Henry Dana, Emily Dickinson, George Plimpton, the Dow Chemical family, Julie Harris and Margaret Mead. 'The more you dig, the smaller the world becomes', the Times reporter who interviewed Reitwiesner observed.

Science writer Guy Murchie, in his book *Seven Mysteries of Life*, argues that we are all related, actually related, as a family. He says that no human being is less related to any other human being than fiftieth cousins. Most of us, he says, are much more closely related. The family trees of all of us meet and merge by the time fifty generations are traced, usually much before. The "family of men", according to Murchie, exists in fact.

In this book and in Dr. Smith's earlier study of the Kallikak family, there has been much criticism of the practice of using genealogical data to support the idea that some families, races, nationalities or social classes

225

are naturally and immodifiably inferior. It is with some trepidation then, that we present some additional family history material on Carrie Buck. We present this information, however, because it so clearly contradicts what was claimed of her genealogy sixty years ago and because of the irony of the story it contains.

Harry Laughlin, in testifying through his disposition, said of Carrie and her family, "These people belong to the shiftless, ignorant, and worthless class of anti-social whites of the South . . . [they are an] ignorant and moving class of people, and it is impossible to get intelligent and satisfactory data." Laughlin found "intelligent and satisfactory" enough, however, the data he submitted to the Circuit Court with apparent confidence that Emma Buck, Carrie's mother, had lived a "life of immorality, prostitution and untruthfulness; has never been self sustaining, was maritally unworthy; having been divorced from her husband on account of infidelity . . . has had one illegitimate child and probably two others inclusive of Carrie Buck . . ."

These comments could have been challenged by Carrie's appointed defense attorney. They were not. Irving Whitehead could have found concrete evidence to refute at least some of these allegations. A trip to the Clerk of Court's Office in Charlottesville, for example, would have resolved the question of Carrie's legitimacy. Had he checked there he would have found that Frank and Emma Buck were married in 1896. There is no record in Charlottesville or Albemarle County of their having been divorced. A check of Carrie's records at the Colony would also have revealed important information about Carrie's father. The family history section of her records there contains the following entry:

"Father, Frank Buck, accidentally killed."

The records shows, then, that Emma Buck was a widow with several children. This may help explain Carrie's placement in a foster home. Emma Buck may have been a "loose" woman. However, the death of her husband may have been an important factor in the outcome of her life and the dissolution of her family.

When reading the original court records of *Buck v. Priddy*, it seems strange that so little emphasis was actually placed on the Buck family. The family history material presented in court concerned Carrie's mother's family. There is a reference in the material suggesting that because she may have been illegitimate Carrie may not have been related to the Bucks. This is a claim of course that could be made at any juncture of anyone's hereditary. As we now know also, there is absolutely nothing to indicate that Carrie was illegitimate. Even with the reference to possible illegitimacy it seems incredible that Estabrook, Laughlin, Priddy and Strode would have overlooked the importance of saying something about the Buck family in the presentation of the case.

Carrie's grandparents were married in Albemarle County. Fleming N. Buck married Athelia Wheat on January 8, 1856. His parents are recorded in the marriage register as being James and M. B. Buck. Fleming's occupation was farming.

James R. Buck, Carrie's great grandfather, was a man of means. The Albemarle County Will Book #26 lists his property as of February 4, 1861. He was a wealthy man with considerable land and financial resources. He owned four slaves. Likewise, Will Book #27 shows that Fleming Buck was prosperous and also the owner of slaves.

A clue to the journey from the wealth of James and Fleming Buck, to the modest means of Carrie's father as a tinner, to the impoverishment of her mother may be found in some of the legal records in the Albemarle County Courthouse. Chancery Orders Book #6 shows that in 1868, when the economy and culture of the area would have been floundering in the wake of the Civil War, James R. Buck went to court to contest the sale of lands by his family. The defendants included "the widow of Fleming N. Buck and his infant heirs Frank Buck, George Buck . . ." The case was apparently a bitter land dispute that ended in an order that the land be sold and the proceeds distributed among the defendants. This could have been the beginning of the end of the family's apparent history of cohesion. There followed numerous *Buck v. Buck* suits in the late 1860's, almost always involving land disputes.

Deed Book #69 in the Albemarle County Courthouse contains a record which may be an important link between Carrie's branch of the Buck family and other Buck ancestors. January 7, 1875 James G. Buck, Patricia Maddox and Sallie Buck Maddox agreed to the sale of the estate of James R. Buck. They signed the agreement and it was notarized in Missouri.

There is a manuscript in the Manuscripts Division of the Alderman Library at the University of Virginia entitled *A Family Migration*. It was written by Walter H. Buck and describes the movements of some branches of a prominent Virginia family, the Bucks. In the manuscript he discussed one branch which moved to Missouri. Some members moved back to Virginia and correspondence was maintained between the Virginia and Missouri groups for years. With more genealogical research a connection might be found, perhaps through Missouri, between Carrie Buck and one of the most prominent families in Virginia's history.

Walter Buck was a prolific and persistent genealogist. In his book *The Buck Family and its Kin* he made the following statement:

> Our family and its kin go back to the earliest days in America and can be traced back with accuracy; though early records are often scanty.
>
> Thomas Buck [sometimes spelled Bucke] came to Virginia on the ship "George" in 1635. The Lee's came in 1640, the Carter's in 1649 and the Byrd's in 1670.

Buck obviously intended by this statement to show that the Bucks were one of the *first* of the First Families of Virginia. His book describes the illustrious past of that family. It is interesting that one major branch of the family lived and built estates around the Front Royal area, the same community where Carrie and Doris later lived in abject poverty.

In an earlier version of the book, *The Buck Family of Virginia*, Walter Buck opened with a different kind of statement:

> When Shakespeare put into the mouth of one of his most amusing characters the boast—'We came

in with Richard Conqueror'—he called attention to a common, human feeling. Family histories are apt to make excessive claims and at the same time to be deficient in the supporting evidence.

This little sketch of our family from its earliest days in Virginia may perhaps be subject to this same criticism. But considering the generally unsatisfactory state of the Virginia records, there is, I think, enough authentic material about our family to justify the preparation of this small volume.

We have already seen the effect of excessive claims about heredity in this book. Of course, the excessiveness we have seen was of negative claims rather than the gilded ones Mr. Buck was cautioning against. Looking only at the evidence of Carrie's direct and immediate ancestors, the irony is sobering. One feels a blend of sadness and bitterness: a terrible sadness at the inaccuracies made of Carrie's heritage and life, an immense bitterness at the things that were done to Carrie and so many others in the name of such theories of human inferiority and superiority.

In 1938 Dr. G. B. Arnold of the State Colony for Epileptics and Feebleminded read a paper on sterilization to the Sixty-second Annual Meeting of the American Association on Mental Deficiency. The paper was a review of the first one thousand people who had been sterilized at the Colony. After giving a brief history of the enactment of Virginia' sterilization statute and *Buck v. Bell*, Arnold made some surprising statements concerning fatalities from sterilization surgery. Proponents of sterilization had repeatedly argued that the procedures were safe; that they posed practically no physical risks to the person being sterilized. Dr. Arnold's remarks indicate otherwise:

> I wish that I could truthfully say that in this series of one thousand cases there had been neither complications nor mortalities—but, I am sorry to report, we have had both.
>
> Quite frequently our patients have removed their bandages within the first twenty-four to thirty-six hours after operation. That superficial infections have resulted from this exploratory curiosity is certainly not to be marveled at.
>
> . . . We positively will not operate unless we are convinced that the patient is a good surgical risk.
>
> We have had two fatalities, both women. The first case to die following the operation was a girl around fifteen years of age. She was operated upon one morning. A general anesthetic [drop ether] was used, and she did not take the anesthesia particularly well. At one time she became quite cyanotic. But she seemed to be getting along reasonably well until that afternoon, when it was noticed that her pulse was very rapid, and her breathing was labored. Her condition improved in the early evening, and she seemed out of danger. However, quite suddenly, at 11:30 that night, she died.
>
> . . . The other case died several hours after the administration of the anesthesia and without ever regaining consciousness. We were unable to get per-

mission for a post-mortem examination, unfortunately, so I cannot say, with absolute certainty, just what caused the second death.

Arnold reported, however, that he found it a pleasure to tell the assembly that of the 607 females and 391 males "who successfully survived" the operation, none had children after being sterilized. He added that those being sterilized were not of extremely low intelligence. Only those who could be placed outside the Colony following the surgery were selected. He also stated that those who were "markedly deteriorated and demented" were not considered good candidates. Arnold made it very clear that those targeted for the operation were "high grade defectives". He also admitted that there had been problems with confusion over the designations "immoral" and "mental deficient." Apparently it had become increasingly common for welfare workers instrumental in committing persons to the Colony to regard the two as being synonymous.

Dr. Arnold argued, however, that sterilization at the Colony had served, up to that point, a sound eugenic purpose. Then, he presented the kind of evidence that had been used to determine the presence of bad genetic traits in those first one thousand people sterilized at the Lynchburg facility.

In our first thousand cases, an even five hundred of them had definitely bad family histories. Two hundred thirty-three of that number had at least one ancestor in the direct or collateral lines who was suffering from some mental disease or defect. Two hundred sixty-seven had more than one . . . (defective) ancestor. No family history was obtainable in one hundred fifty-three of the one thousand. Three hundred forty-seven of the patients had, so far as we could ascertain, no demonstrable . . . (defective) ancestor.

Across America, thousands of so-called "mentally defective" people have been sterilized due to Carrie Buck's case. Hundreds of people had been sterilized in the first decade following Carrie's case on the basis of having *one* ancestor who somebody had judged to be defective! Others were sterilized on no evidence of negative genetic traits at all. With apparently no qualms, Arnold asked his listeners to "bear in mind that the histories in several hundred of these cases were not nearly so complete as we would desire; yet, in spite of that fact, we *know* that 50 percent of these one thousand patients had a definitely bad family history."

After stating that most of the people who had been sterilized had come from small towns or rural areas, Arnold spoke directly to the social and economic backgrounds of these people.

Eight hundred and twelve of them came from families of the definitely low class—and by 'low class' we mean families whose heads are barely ekeing out an existence; those who are unable to save anything against the inevitable rainy day, but who are not, in anything approximating normal times, ordinarily on the relief roles.

A final part of the formula for those who were sterilized was the factor of unacceptable sexual behavior.

> Four hundred and four of the women had been guilty of sexual immorality prior to admission . . . Seventy-nine of our patients (both male and female) averaged four illegitimate children. One hundred thirty-nine of our patients (one hundred thirty-eight of them women) had two hundred-one illegitimate children.

In his address to the convention, Arnold revealed the criteria which, perhaps not entirely conscious and, in that sense, not completely intentional, were actually operative in the selection of people for institutionalization and sterilization. Those who were at greater risk were, like Carrie, young and poor. They were likely to come from small communities where their misbehavior was more likely to stand out and where advocates were more difficult to find. They were considered, for one reason or another, to come from "bad stock." Finally, their misbehavior was likely to have been sexual in nature and may have resulted in an illegitimate birth.

Young women were the most common victims of this profile, but, as we have seen, men were also sterilized for these same reasons. Buck Smith's story is a good example.

Buck was born in Richmond to a couple who could not support him. He lived his first eight years in various city institutions. For reasons he does not understand, he was sent to the Colony. He was sterilized there when he was fifteen years old. He told his story in 1980 to a reporter from the *Roanoke Times and World News*.

"They separated us according to ability," Smith recalled. "Most of the kids seemed to come from broken homes. There wasn't to my mind, that many retarded. They were just sort of lost . . . Eventually, you knew your time would come. Everybody knew it. A lot of us just joked about it. There was a lot of kidding and joking. We weren't growed up enough to think about it. We didn't know what it meant."

Buck recalled that one day a group of boys and girls met in the basement of one of the buildings:

"We were just beginning to find out what life was all about," Smith said, explaining that some sexual activity took place.

"Then the girls told on us," he said, "and they put me in confinement for a month. They said I had to be taught a lesson. Two weeks later they came to me and told me they were going to have to sterilize me."

Buck went on to describe his recollections of the sterilization procedure and of his departure from the institution a short time later. He was married at age 18. That marriage ended in divorce after thirteen years. He felt that his wife was unable to accept the fact that they could not have children, and yet could not bring herself to talk with him about her feelings. Buck remarried shortly afterward to a woman who had two children by a previous husband. The newspaper article in which Buck told his story closed with his expression of regret at not having children of his own:

"Having children is supposed to be part of the human race. Sometimes I feel like there's a part that I'm missing." Tears swelled up in his eyes, surrounded by creases of a life of hard work.

ILLUSTRATION 10: Picture captioned "Epileptic Mother and Feeble Minded Children." Fifth Annual Report, Virginia State Epileptic Colony, Lynchburg, Virginia.

Behind him, pasted to a mirror, was a dollar bill Smith said might bring him luck. And below that was a card from his stepchildren.

'Thinking of you Daddy' it reads. 'They call me Daddy,' Smith said."

Another example of the sterilizations that occurred following Carrie's case is the story of Sallie Johnson Wilcher.

In 1929, Sallie's two-year-old son was taken from her. He was illegitimate and was taken away by social workers. She would never see her son again.

Sally was committed to the Colony and was sterilized. She spent nine months in the institution. In an interview with Mary Bishop, a newspaper reporter, she recalled sitting in a corner and crying while there. When she was asked why she didn't try to escape, she described a small and frightening solitary cell where runaways were placed. She also remembered that when girls ran away and were brought back, they were given vaginal douches to "clean 'em out because they might have been with a man."

Sallie's experience with the Colony was similar to Carrie's. She was paroled first to a family where she cooked and cleaned. She was then moved to a boarding-house where she cooked for seventeen boarders. She was finally discharged after she married. She had been the wife of Voyd Wilcher since 1942. Voyd was a retired timber cutter.

Sallie wanted more than anything else to find her son. On the day in 1929 when Sallie left her home in a car with the social workers, they dropped her off at the

Colony and told her they were taking her child to Richmond. When they picked her up she was told that they were taking her to a "home" and she thought her son would be left with her there. For over fifty years, Sallie wondered about the son she had named William Lee Johnson. She told Mary Bishop that she had always wanted to know where he was. She explained that she didn't want him to know anything about her; she was afraid that he would be hurt by knowledge of his origins. But she longed for a chance to see him.

Sallie told the reporter that she would have liked to have had other children.

" 'Now, I wouldn't have minded having more children,' she said. 'Like I said, they took my baby away from me and made it so I couldn't have no more' . . . 'I didn't know what they was doing to me,' Wilcher said. 'I still have my scar.' "

In September of 1987, Mary Bishop telephoned Dr. Smith. She was planning a series of articles on sterilization, had read Dr. Smith's book *Minds Made Feeble*, and wanted to discuss the history of eugenics in Virginia. Mary met Dr. Smith later that day. She shared with him that afternoon a second article she had written about Sallie Wilcher a year and a half after the first.

In the second article Bishop explained that Sallie allowed her to interview her initially in the hope that, somehow, the publicity from the story would help her find her son. The only response Sallie got to the story, however, was from a writer interested in doing a screenplay. She signed a contract and was told she would share the proceeds if he sold the idea. She never heard from him again.

Mary Bishop was disappointed that the story had not helped Sallie and she decided to try to assist her more directly in her search for her son. Sallie had learned from a Legal Aid attorney that her son had been adopted in 1932 in Raleigh, North Carolina. The couple who had adopted him were named Lamkin. He had been renamed William Everett Lamkin. He had died in 1973.

Mary learned from old Raleigh directories that William's adoptive father was a traveling salesman. The family's last listed neighborhood had been torn down. People listed as their neighbors couldn't be found. A bit of encouragement came when a worker with Social Security confirmed that William had children, that Sallie Wilcher was a grandmother. The worker could not, however, provide information on how many, how old, or where the children were. Encouraged, Mary Bishop went to Raleigh and researched court records, police records, death certificates, and real estate, utility, and tax records. She found nothing.

An inquiry to another Social Security worker, Carl Watson, offered new hope. Watson could not reveal the names and addresses of William's family but agreed that he would forward a letter from Sallie to the last address of any survivors of her son.

On July 8, 1986 Sallie got a call from Sue Lamkin of Hampton, Virginia. She had married William in 1959. She told Sallie that she had three grandsons.

Some time later Sallie received a letter from Sue Lamkin with pictures of William as a little boy and as a man. There was also a picture of William with his sons when they were small. She responded by sending the Lamkins pictures of herself, and she decided to go to see her grandchildren in Hampton. Her intention to make that trip would not be realized. In January of 1987, while being driven to see a physician, Sallie began to slur as she spoke and slumped over in her seat. That day she suffered several strokes. She died in the hospital the next morning. Sallie was seventy-six years old.

Following Sallie's death, Mary Bishop contacted her daughter-in-law.

> I called Sue Lamkin last week and told her about Sallie's death. 'Oh no, that's too bad,' she said. She'd been planning to write again soon. She and her sister were thinking about driving up to see Sallie next summer. 'I really wanted to meet her.' "
>
> 'At Christmas,' she said, 'the family got together and she passed around Sallie's letter and the newspaper article' [Sallie had sent a copy of Mary Bishop's first article about her].

Over the phone she answered some questions Sallie never got to ask.

The grandsons, William, Clyde and Lloyd, were now 26, 22, and 21 years old. One worked in an iron plant in Maryland, another at a Hampton asphalt company and the youngest, an auto body whiz, at a Tidewater junkyard.

Sue Lamkin said that her husband did not know that he had been adopted until 1965. Perhaps because of the sensitivity to the persisting legacy of eugenics, someone told him that at the time of his birth his mother was a college coed and his father was a professor. He was told he came from "good blood."

16

The Persistent Solution

---

*I*n 1939 Dr. J. S. DeJarnette wrote to Aubrey Strode thanking him for a speech he had made at a gathering in honor of DeJarnette. The occasion had marked his fiftieth year with Virginia's system of mental institutions. His remarks portray not only his esteem for Strode but also his continuing enthusiasm for sterilization.

> I want to thank you for the splendid address you made at my fiftieth anniversary celebration. It was kind of you and Mrs. Strode to come.
>
> I can hark back many years when I first knew you.

I had heard you speak in the Senate and had your cooperation in the great sterilization law of the United States. We can call it the United States law because it was the first law of the kind ever approved by the United States Court of Appeals.

If you had never done anything else you would have done more for your State than any one man in it. We have sterilized in Virginia 3300 and we estimate that in 100 years we will have saved the State of Virginia over four hundred million dollars. At the same time we are raising the mentality of our people and saving suffering, murder, accidents, crime—and the greatest crime of all is allowing the feeble-minded people to raise children in a feeble-minded environment.

I wish to thank you again for attending and participating in my anniversary celebration, and I hope you will allow me to call you my friend.

Following Aubrey Strode's death, his widow, Louisa, asked Dr. Dejarnette to write a letter concerning Strode's contribution to the sterilization statute to an editor who was collecting information for a biographical listing. By that time the sterilization rolls had grown, as had De-Jarnette's belief in the efficacy of the eugenics movement of which he had for so long been a part. DeJarnette was writing these words in 1947 at the same time that the Nazi atrocities which had been committed under the rubric of eugenics were being revealed to the world.

Our Virginia law is both humane and economical, and is destined to save millions in dollars and more

242

in accidents, crimes, disgrace, suffering and poverty and eventually to raise our standard of intelligence. Under the Virginia law the sterilized individual can go out into the world, marry and live his sexual life with no danger of adding to the burdens of society or of lowering the intelligence of the nation.

The Virginia law on sexual sterilization was the first sterilization law to stand the rest of the United States Court of Appeals in the celebrated case of *Buck v. Bell*. The people of Virginia are and should be eternally grateful to . . . (Aubrey) Strode for giving this legislative masterpiece to humanity. Already Virginia has sterilized over 5,300 and is next to California in the United States in sterilizations.

Senator Strode possessed a wonderful personality and was greatly beloved and honored by his State. I am proud to have been numbered among his good friends. I loved and revered him.

By the time he wrote this letter DeJarnette was retired. He signed the letter over the titles of "Former Superintendent, Western State Hospital" and "Founder and Builder, DeJarnette State Sanatorium." Dr. DeJarnette was obviously proud of his role in the development of the facilities, policies and practices of the state hospital system. As he acknowledged, he participated in the construction of a facility which was to be, and is, a monument to him. He constructed his own monument as well on the issue of eugenics. In his 1920 report from Western State Hospital he included his conception of the importance of race improvement.

Mendel's Law: A Plea For A Better Race Of Men

Oh, why are you men so foolish—
  You breeders who breed our men
Let the fools, the weaklings and crazy
  Keep breeding and breeding again?
The criminal, deformed, and the misfit,
  Dependent, diseased, and the rest—
As we breed the human family
  The worst is as good as the best.

Go to the house of some farmer,
  Look through his barns and sheds,
Look at his horses and cattle,
  Even his hogs are thoroughbreds;
Then look at his stamp on his children,
  Low browed with the monkey jaw,
Ape handed, and silly, and foolish—
  Bred true to Mendel's law.

Go to some homes in the village,
  Look at the garden beds,
The cabbage, the lettuce and turnips,
  Even the beets are thoroughbreds.
Then look at the many children
  With hands like the monkey's paw,
Bowlegged, flatheaded, and foolish—
  Bred true to Mendel's law.
This is the law of Mendel,
  And often he makes it plain,
Defectives will breed defectives
  And the insane breed insane.
Oh, why do we allow these people

To breed back to the monkey's nest,
To increase our country's burdens
 When we should breed for the good and the best.

Oh, you wise men take up the burden,
 And make this your loudest creed,
Sterilize the misfits promptly—
 All not fit to breed.
Then our race will be strengthened and bettered,
 And our men and women blest,
Not apish, repulsive and foolish,
 For we should breed from the good and the best.

The number of voices speaking as enthusiastically in favor of eugenic sterilization as DeJarnette were rare even in the heyday of its popularity. Following World War II, there was a very dramatic decline in the number and volume of these voices. This decline was due in large part to the realization in scientific and intellectual circles of the awful truth of the Holocaust. The uses to which eugenic philosophy had been put in Nazi Germany shocked some who had advocated the same philosophy in the United States. Those who continued to believe in the tenets of eugenics were generally more careful and quiet in their advocacy of genetic solutions to social problems. The eugenic sterilization movement was dormant, however, not dead. It would continue to be manifested for many years to come.

In 1965, Sheldon and Elizabeth Reed of the University of Minnesota produced a voluminus work entitled *Mental Retardation: A Family Study.* The book contained information on over 80,000 people, all of them relatives of a group of 289 residents of the Faribault State School and Colony in Minnesota who had first been studied in 1911. The original study had been conducted under the auspices of the Eugenics Record Office. For that study two people were trained as field workers at the Office and were then assigned to Faribault. From 1911 to 1918 they collected family histories, conducted interviews and constructed pedigrees on the original 289 subjects. The study was reopened in 1949, and the Reeds traced the descendents until 1965.

The book is an amazing document. It contains page after page of family charts that are simply extensions of those developed by the early workers at the Eugenics Record Office. The manner in which people are described is reminiscent of the Kallikak study and the family history of Carrie Buck. After discussing how their study was conducted and summarizing their findings, the Reeds present some rather sweeping conclusions:

> We end our discussion with the perhaps euphoric opinion that the intelligence of the population is increasing slowly, and that greater protection of the retarded from reproduction will augment the rate of gain. The elevation of the average intelligence is essential for the comprehension of our increasingly complicated world.

The Reeds' view was, obviously, that institutionalization was resulting in an overall gain of intelligence in the population and that, as more defective people were prevented from reproducing, the gain would be increased. The Reeds felt that a significant "humanitarian" aspect of their study was that it demonstrated that a better legal basis should be provided for the sterilization of "higher grade retardates" in the community. They went beyond the argument that sterilization should be used to prevent hereditary problems. "Few people have emphasized that where the transmission of a trait is frequently from parent to offspring, sterilization would be effective and it is irrelevant whether the basis for the trait is genetic or environmental." The Reeds were advocating the concept that problems of environment, as well as those of heredity, could be improved with this technique. Taken literally—and there is no indication that the reader is expected to do otherwise—they were arguing that the problem of poverty could be resolved by sterilizing the poor, the problem of ignorance could be remedied by sterilizing the ignorant—the socially therapeutic applications of sterilization seem limitless!

The Reed's vision of the positive effects of sterilization was expressed in one of their summary statements:

> When voluntary sterilization for the retarded becomes a part of the culture of the United States, we should expect a decrease of about 50 percent per generation in the number of retarded.

A staggering percentage decrease, if possible; and an appealing idea for those seeking a seemingly fast and easy way of "curing" a major social ill. It must be remembered, however, that the Reeds' claim for the efficacy of

247

sterilization sounds like an echo of the arguments made forty years earlier in a Virginia courtroom.

One of the earliest books on ecology was written by William Vogt and published in 1948. Vogt had been much influenced by eugenics: in *Road to Survival*, he applied the ideas of the economist Thomas Malthus to natural resources and conservation. The central theme of the book was that overpopulation posed the greatest single threat to our exhaustive supply of natural resources and, thereby, to economic and social stability worldwide. Vogt argued that, only by curbing population growth in "backward cultures" and in the lower classes of all societies, would humankind survive. He proposed harsh measures through which to control population. Vogt opposed, for example, foreign aid that would provide food and medical care to China or India. He felt that a high death rate in such countries was a "national asset." He thought that death should be allowed to do its work in bringing population growth under control. Vogt also offered some observations on sterilization. He provided one suggestion that was to find support some years later.

> There is more than little merit in the suggestion . . . of small but adequate amounts of money to be paid to anyone—especially the males—who would agree to the simple sterilization operation . . . Since such a bonus would appeal primarily to the world's shiftless, it would probably have a favorable selective influence. From the point of view of society, it would certainly be preferable to pay permanent indigent individuals, many of whom would be physically and psychologically marginal, $50 or $100

rather than support their hordes of offspring that, by both genetic and social inheritance, would tend to perpetuate the fikleness.

In 1956, William Shockley was awarded the Nobel Prize for Physics. The award came as a result of his work with Bell Laboratories in the development of the transistor. Shockley has held teaching and research positions in several major universities. Today, however, he is known less for his accomplishments in physics than for his views on race and intelligence.

Shockley argues that intelligence is largely hereditary and that the black race is innately inferior in intellect. Like many of the earlier eugenicists, Shockley has no credentials in genetics, nor does he have any background in the social sciences. He simply began to voice his views on intelligence, genetics, and race; and many people have listened receptively.

In the mid-seventies, Shockley proposed a "thinking exercise" about sterilization which was published in the book *Eugenics: Then and Now.* He hoped the exercise would stimulate thinking about dealing with the problems created by inherited defects in intelligence. His plan involved the award of cash bonuses to people who scored low on intelligence tests and agreed to be sterilized:

> At a bonus rate of $1,000 for each point below 100 I.Q., $30,000 put in trust for a 70 I.Q. moron potentially capable of producing 20 children might return $250,000 to taxpayers in reduced costs of mental retardation care. Ten percent of the bonus in spot

cash might put our national talent for entrepreneur-
ship into action.

Note should be made that Shockley's connection
with old-line eugenics is evident even in his use of the
term moron. Most other contemporary hereditarians appear to avoid being identified with what might be considered the historical excesses of the movement. Shockley
speaks unabashed of eugenics, dysgenics, and morons.

In his sterilization proposal, Shockley anticipates
the problem of reaching those who must need to have the
surgery done:

> A feature that might frustrate the plan is that
> those who are not bright enough to learn of the
> bonus on their own are the ones most important to
> reach. The problem of reaching such people is what
> might be solved by paying the 10 percent of the
> bonus in spot cash.
>
> Bounty hunters attracted by getting a cut of the
> bonus might then persuade low I.Q., high-bonus
> types to volunteer.

In a 1980 interview Shockley referred to Elmer Pendell, the demographer, who argues that civilizations decline when "problem makers" multiply at a greater rate
than "problem solvers." In his book, *Sex Versus Civilization*, Pendell proposes a law that would prevent the marriage and reproduction of problem makers. Among those
that Pendell would not allow to marry unless sterilized
would be "those who cannot earn a living" and "those of
very low I.Q.'s or less than four years of education."

In his book, Pendell illustrates the potential power of a simple idea combined with a convincing teacher. In a college class he taught on population, he covered various propositions for controlling the growth of a population or of certain portions of a population. The propositions included sterilization, limitations on immigration and restrictive marriage laws. Near the end of the semester Pendell handed out ballots and gave each student the opportunity to vote for or against each of these measures. The results he reported are startling; 88 percent of the students were in favor of increased restrictions on immigration, 76 percent were in favor of laws restricting marriage, and 73 percent supported the idea of a bonus plan to encourage sterilization. This is but another example of the power and persistence of eugenic concepts. It also illustrates the social amnesia which seems to occur regarding the tragedies that these concepts have engendered in the past.

In 1980 a lawsuit was brought by the American Civil Liberties Union on behalf of the 8,300 men and women who had been sterilized in Virginia institutions before the practice was officially ceased in 1974. One of the petitioners in that suit was Doris Buck. Unlike Carrie, she had not forgiven, nor had she forgotten her persecutors. Doris wanted to be compensated for the pain and suffering she had for so long endured because others had wrested rightful choices for her life away from her. According to the suit, thousands of the residents of those institutions, like Doris, were sexually sterilized without proper explanation of the effects of the operation. The claim was also made that in many instances the residents were not told they were being sterilized, and were not given the necessary psychological and medical assistance in connection with the sterilizations.

In 1985 a settlement was approved by the United States District Court for the Western District of Virginia. The terms of the settlement provided for a media campaign to notify former residents of state institutions that they could inquire and be informed whether they had been sterilized. The settlement also provided for psychological counseling for persons who were sterilized against their will or without their knowledge—seemingly small restitution for a great injustice.

The hearing of this suit generated nationwide news coverage. A major network tried to land a helicopter on Doris Figgin's front yard in order to get a private interview. The saga even made the *New Delhi Times* in India. It stimulated many of the newspaper stories mentioned earlier, including the interview with Doris Buck Figgans. A shocking revelation surfaced: across America fifty thousand people, termed mentally ill or retarded, had been sterilized after the Supreme Court rendered its decision in Carrie Buck's case. The laws which governed these sterilizations were based on the law enacted in the State of Virginia.

It might be reasonably assumed that the case and the associated news coverage would have made public officials very sensitive to the issue of sterilization. Involuntary sexual sterilization was, however, to prove to be persistent as an expedient solution to complex social problems.

In 1986 a member of the Virginia Board of Social

Services suggested that welfare mothers should be sterilized to help break the welfare cycle among the poor. The board member, a former state treasurer and legislator, presented his views to members of the General Assembly in a letter advocating sterilization as the "best solution." After a newspaper account of his letter caused a short-lived controversy, the official apologized for any embarrassment he had caused other board members but added that he had received quite a number of favorable responses to his letter from members of the General Assembly committees that deal with welfare issues. He added that he had only hoped "to arouse some thoughts and ideas which might lead to a positive program."

Almost sixty years after Carrie Buck was sterilized, the same simple and erroneous sermon was being offered to both politicians and the public. The eugenic falsehood which scarred Carrie's life is frighteningly resilient. It outlived Carrie Buck. It outlived the Holocaust. It resides in the consciousness and values of many otherwise reasonable and decent people. One hopes the haunting images of Carrie Buck, of her tragic life and triumphant spirit, will help us to resist the appeal of dangerously simple answers to painfully complex human questions. That became increasingly true for us as we wrote this book. We hope that, in some measure, the same is true for you having read it.

Bibliography

Act of March 20 (1924). *Acts of Assembly* Chap. 394, pp. 569–570.

Anonymous. (1927). May 4 postcard to J. H. Bell. Carrie Buck File, Central Virginia Training Center, Lynchburg, Virginia.

Arnold, G. B. (1938). "A brief review of the first thousand patients eugenically sterilized at the State Colony for Epileptics and Feebleminded." *American Association on Mental Deficiency Proceedings.* Vol. 43, pp. 56–63.

———. (1940). October 29 letter to Carrie (Buck) Eagle. Carrie Buck File, Central Virginia Training Center, Lynchburg, Virginia.

Bell, J. H. (1923). April 3 letter to Caroline Wilhelm. Carrie Buck File, Central Virginia Training Center, Lynchburg, Virginia.

———. (1925). February 13 letter to A. E. Strode. Carrie Buck File, Central Virginia Training Center, Lynchburg, Virginia.

———. (1928a). January 12 letter to Mrs. J. T. Dobbs. Carrie Buck File, Central Virginia Training Center, Lynchburg, Virginia.

———. (1928b). February 14 letter to Mrs. J. T. Dobbs. Carrie Buck File, Central Virginia Training Center, Lynchburg, Virginia.

———. (1928c). February 20 letter to Mrs. A. T. Newberry. Carrie Buck File, Central Virginia Training Center, Lynchburg, Virginia.

———. (1928d). February 22 letter to Mrs. A. J. Newberry, Carrie Buck File, Central Virginia Training Center, Lynchburg, Virginia.

———. (1928e). August 16 letter to Carrie Buck. Carrie Buck File, Central Virginia Training Center, Lynchburg, Virginia.

———. (1928f). December 11 letter to Mrs. A. T. Newberry. Carrie Buck File, Central Virginia Training Center, Lynchburg, Virginia.

———. (1930). undated letter to Carrie (Buck) Eagle. Carrie Buck File, Central Virginia Training Center, Lynchburg, Virginia.

———. (1933a). March 31 letter to Carrie Buck. Carrie Buck File, Central Virginia Training Center, Lynchburg, Virginia.

———. (1933b). August 2 letter to Carrie Buck. Carrie Buck File, Central Virginia Training Center, Lynchburg, Virginia.

Bishop, M. (1985). June 30 "Sallie Johnson wasn't retarded but they sterilized her anyway." *Ronaoke*

Times and World News, Roanoke, Virginia, pp. A-1, A-9.

———. (1987). January 25 "Life's quest: Sallie held onto hope of finding kin." *Roanoke Times and World News*, Ronaoke, Virginia, pp. A-1, A-11.

Booker, B. (1981, February 27). "Nazi Sterilizations had their roots in U.S. eugenics." *Richmond Times-Dispatch*, Richmond, Virginia pp. A1, A6.

Buck, Carrie (1928a). August 2 letter to Mrs. Berry. Carrie Buck File, Central Virginia Training Center, Lynchburg, Virginia.

———. (1928b). December 8 letter to J. H. Bell. Carrie Buck File, Central Virginia Training Center, Lynchburg, Virginia.

———. (1930). December 14 letter to Dr. J. H. Bell. Carrie Buck File, Central Virginia Training Center, Lynchburg, Virginia.

———. (1940). October 22 letter to Dr. J. B. Arnold. Carrie Buck File, Central Virginia Training Center, Lynchburg, Virginia.

Buck v. Bell. (1927). 274 U.S. 200, 47 S. Ct. 584.

Buck v. Priddy (1924). Amherst County Clerk of Courts Office, Amherst County Courthouse, Amherst, Virginia.

Buck, Walter H. (undated). A Family Migration (Collection #4938). Manuscripts Division, University of Virginia Library, Charlottesville, Virginia.

———. (1956). *The Buck Family and Its Kin*. Baltimore: Schneidereith and Sons.

———. (1936). *The Buck Family of Virginia*. Baltimore: Schneidereith and Sons.

Carrie Buck Record. (1924). Carrie Buck File, Central Virginia Training Center, Lynchburg, Virginia.

Cattell, J., Editor (1949). *American Men of Science: A Biographical Directory* (Eighth Edition). Lancaster, Pennsylvania: The Science Press.

Coleman, M. M. (Mr.) (1928). January 5 letter to Dr. J. H. Bell. Carrie Buck File, Central Virginia Training Center, Lynchburg, Virginia.

Coleman, M. M. (Mrs). (1927). December 19 letter to J. H. Bell. Carrie Buck File, Central Virginia Training Center, Lynchburg, Virginia.

———. (1928). January 5 letter to J. H. Bell. Carrie Buck File, Central Virginia Training Center, Lynchburg, Virginia.

Compton, J. (1987). May 25 letter to J. D. Smith. Author's file, Lynchburg, Virginia.

The Daily Advance (1980). "Case Led To Sterilization Law," February 27, 1980 *The Daily Advance*, Lynchburg, Virginia, p. 24.

Davenport, C. (1911). January 8 letter to A. H. Estabrook. Charles Davenport Collection, American Philosophical Society Library, Philadelphia, Pennsylvania.

———. (1912a). May 16 letter to A. H. Estabrook. Charles Davenport Collection, American Philosophical Society Library, Philadelphia, Pennsylvania.

———. (1912b). December 29 letter to A. H. Estabrook. Charles Davenport Collection, American Philosophical Society Library, Philadelphia, Pennsylvania.

———. (1923). March 5 letter to A. H. Estabrook. Charles Davenport Collection, American Philosophical Society Library, Philadelphia, Pennsylvania.

———. (1924). November 21 letter to A. H. Estabrook.

Charles Davenport Collection, American Philosophical Society Library, Philadelphia, Pennsylvania.

———. (1928). November 28 letter to Mrs. Estabrook. Charles Davenport Collection, American Philosophical Society Library, Philadelphia, Pennsylvania.

DeJarnette, J. S. (1920). *Report of the Western State Hospital*. Staunton, Virginia.

———. (1939). July 24 letter to Aubrey Strode. Box 154, Aubrey Strode Collection, Manuscripts Department, University of Virginia Library, Charlottesville, Virginia.

———. (1947). October 24 letter to John Dickson. "Additional Papers." Aubrey Strode Collection, Manuscripts Department, University of Virginia Library, Charlottesville, Virginia.

Dobbs, J. T. (Mrs.). (1928). February 13 letter to J. H. Bell. Carrie Buck File, Central Virginia Training Center, Lynchburg, Virginia.

Eagle, C. (1932). May 17 letter to J. H. Bell. Carrie Buck File, Central Virginia Training Center, Lynchburg, Virginia.

———. (1933a). March 27 letter to Dr. J. H. Bell. Carrie Buck File, Central Virginia Training Center, Lynchburg, Virginia.

———. (1933b). August 19 letter to J. H. Bell. Carrie Buck File, Central Virginia Training Center, Lynchburg, Virginia.

———. (1933c). April letter to J. H. Bell. Carrie Buck File, Central Virginia Training Center, Lynchburg, Virginia.

Estabrook, A. H. (no date a). Letter fragment, Box 57, Aubrey Strode Collection, Manuscripts Department,

University of Virginia Library, Charlottesville, Virginia.

———. (no date b). Letter fragment, Box 57, Aubrey Strode Collection, Manuscripts Department, University of Virginia Library, Charlottesville, Virginia.

———. (1912). May 15 letter to C. Davenport. Charles Davenport Collection, American Philosophical Society Library, Philadelphia, Pennsylvania.

———. (1913). November 22 letter to Harry Laughlin. Charles Davenport Collection, American Philosophical Society Library, Philadelphia, Pennsylvania.

———. (1923a). January 28 letter to Charles Davenport, Charles Davenport Collection, BD 27, American Philosophical Society Library, Philadelphia, Pennsylvania.

———. (1923b). February 10 letter to Louisa Hubbard. Aubrey Strode Collection, Box 57, Manuscripts Department, University of Virginia Library, Charlottesville, Virginia.

———. (1923c). August 4 letter to Charles Davenport. Charles Davenport Collection, American Philosophical Society Library, Philadelphia, Pennsylvania.

———. (1924). Annual Report for 1923–24 to the Eugenics Record Office. Charles Davenport Collection, American Philosophical Society Library, Philadelphia, Pennsylvania.

———. (1929). June 23 letter to Charles Davenport. Charles Davenport Collection, American Philosophical Society Library, Philadelphia, Pennsylvania.

Estabrook, A. H. & Davenport, C. (1912). *The Nam Family: A Study in Cacogenics*. Cold Spring Harbor, N.Y.: Eugenics Record Office.

Flood, H. D. (1918). April 10 letter to A. E. Strode. Aubrey Strode Collection, Box 30, Manuscripts Department, University of Virginia Library, Charlottesville, Virginia.

Goddard, H. H. (1912). *The Kallikak Family: A Study in the Heredity of Feeble-Mindedness.* New York: Macmillan.

Gould, S. J. (1984). "Carrie Buck's daughter". *Natural History, 93,* 7, 14–18.

Harrell, D. L. (1942). October 23 letter to J. E. Coogen. Carrie Buck File, Central Virginia Training Center, Lynchburg, Virginia.

History of Virginia, Vol. V, Virginia Biography. (1924). New York: The American Historical Society.

Holmes, Oliver Wendell, Jr. (1927). May 19 letter to Lewis Einstein. Oliver Wendell Holmes Jr. Collection, Library of Congress, No. 3451, Box 3.

Holmes, S. J. (1936). *Human Genetics and Its Social Import.* New York: McGraw-Hill.

Houck, P. (1984). *Indian Island in Amherst County.* Lynchburg, Virginia: Lynchburg Historical Research Co.

Hubbard, L. (no date). Handwritten note, Box 57, Aubrey Strode Collection, Manuscripts Department, University of Virginia Library, Charlottesville, Virginia.

———. (1919a). November 17 letter to A. E. Strode. Aubrey Strode Collection, Box 80, Manuscripts Department, University of Virginia Library, Charlottesville, Virginia.

———. (1919b). December 10 letter to A. E. Strode. Aubrey Strode Collection, Box 80, Manuscripts Department, University of Virginia Library, Charlottesville, Virginia.

———. (1919c). December 23 letter to A. E. Strode. Aubrey Strode Collection, Box 80, Manuscripts Department, University of Virginia Library, Charlottesville, Virginia.

———. (1923a). January 28 letter to A. E. Strode. Aubrey Strode Collection, Box 57, Manuscripts Department, University of Virginia Library, Charlottesville, Virginia.

———. (1923b). undated note to A. E. Strode. Aubrey Strode Collection, Box 57, Manuscripts Department, University of Virginia Library, Charlottesville, Virginia.

———. (1923c). September 12 letter to A. E. Strode. Aubrey Strode Collection, Box 57, University of Virginia Library, Charlottesville, Virginia.

———. (1923d). September 20 letter to A. E. Strode. Aubrey Strode Collection, Box 57, University of Virginia Library, Charlottesville, Virginia.

———. (1923e). September 24 letter to A. E. Strode. Aubrey Strode Collection, Box 57, University of Virginia Library, Charlottesville, Virginia.

Hudson, J. D. (1922). January 12 letter to A. E. Strode. Aubrey Strode Collection, Box 148, Manuscripts Department, University of Virginia Library, Charlottesville, Virginia.

Laughlin, H. H. (1922). Eugenical Sterilization in the United States. Chicago: Psychopathic Laboratory of the Municipal Court of Chicago.

———. (1924). October 3 letter to A. E. Strode. Carrie Buck File, Central Virginia Training Center, Lynchburg, Virginia.

———. (1929). The Legal Status of Eugenical Sterilization. Chicago: Psychopathic Laboratory of the Municipal Court of Chicago.

———. (1936a). (May 28 letter to C. Schneider). *Laughlin Notebooks, Vol. II, Nazi Eugenics*. Washington University, St. Louis, Missouri.

———. (1936b). (August 11 letter to C. Schneider). *Laughlin Notebooks, Vol. II, Nazi Eugenics*. Washington University, St. Louis, Missouri.

Layman, J. (1986). January 29 letter to J. David Smith. Author's files.

Lombardo, P. A. (1982). *Eugenic Sterilization In Virginia: Aubrey Strode and the Case of Buck v. Bell*. Dissertation. Charlottesville, Virginia: University of Virginia.

Ludmerer, K. M. (1972). *Genetics and American Society*, Baltimore: Johns Hopkins University Press.

Mallory, G. (1917). November 5 letter to A. S. Priddy, November 5, 1917. "Grounds of Defense, *Willie T. Mallory v. A. S. Priddy*". Virginia State Archive File Drawer #383, item #2711. As cited in Lombardo, P.A. (1982). *Eugenic Sterilization In Virginia: Aubrey Strode And The Case Of Buck v. Bell*. Dissertation. Charlottesville, Virginia: University of Virginia.

McKelway, B. (1980). February 24 "They gave me what life I have and they took a lot of my life away." *Roanoke Times* and *World News*, Roanoke, Virginia, pp. A-1, B-1.

Medical Record (1927). October 19 and November 3 entries. Carrie Buck File, Central Virginia Training Center, Lynchburg, Virginia.

Murchie, G. (1978). *Seven Mysteries of Life*. New York: Houghton Mifflin.

The National Cyclopaedia of American Biography (1948). New York: James T. White & Co.

Newberry, A. T. (1928). February 18 letter to J. H. Bell. Carrie Buck File, Central Virginia Training Center, Lynchburg, Virginia.

———. (1929). January 29 letter to J. H. Bell. Carrie Buck File, Central Virginia Training Center, Lynchburg, Virginia.

Newberry, A. T. (Mrs.) (1928). February 26 letter to J. H. Bell. Carrie Buck File, Central Virginia Training Center, Lynchburg, Virginia.

———. (1928b). February 28 letter to J. H. Bell. Carrie Buck File, Central Virginia Training Center, Lynchburg, Virginia.

———. (1928c). May 25 letter to J. H. Bell. Carrie Buck File, Central Virginia Training Center, Lynchburg, Virginia.

———. (1928d). December 9 letter to J. H. Bell. Carrie Buck File, Central Virginia Training Center, Lynchburg, Virginia.

The News and Daily Advance (1986). May 23 "State Official Regrets Letter On Sterilization." *The News and Daily Advance*, Lynchburg, Virginia, p. C-4.

Pendell, E. (1967). *Sex Versus Civilization*. Los Angeles: Noontide Press.

Plecker, W. A. (1924). Eugenics in Relation to the New Family. Richmond: Virginia State Board of Health.

Popenoe, P. (1934). "The German Sterilization Law." *Journal of Heredity, 25,* 257–264.

Prichard, W. I. (1960). "History of Lynchburg Training School and Hospital". *Mental Health in Virginia, 10(4),* 40–46.

Priddy, A. S. (1910). *Report of the State Epileptic Colony,* Lynchburg, Virginia: State Epileptic Colony.

———. (1911). *Report of the State Epileptic Colony.* Lynchburg, Virginia: State Epileptic Colony.

———. (1915). *Report of the State Epileptic Colony.* Lynchburg, Virginia: State Epileptic Colony.

———. (1917). November 13 letter to George Mallory, November 13, 1917. "Grounds of Defense, *Willie T. Mallory v. A. S. Priddy".* Virginia State Archive File Drawer #383, Item #2711. As cited in Lombardo, P.A. (1982). *Eugenic Sterilization In Virginia: Aubrey Strode And The Case of Buck v. Bell.* Dissertation, Charlottesville, Virginia: University of Virginia.

———. (1923). *Biennial Report of the State Epileptic Colony.* Lynchburg, Virginia: State Epileptic Colony.

———. (1924a). March 13 letter to Homer Richey. Carrie Buck File, Central Virginia Training Center, Lynchburg, Virginia.

———. (1924b). March 14 letter to Caroline Wilhelm. Carrie Buck File, Central Virginia Training Center, Lynchburg, Virginia.

———. (1924c). May 7 letter to Caroline Wilhelm. Carrie Buck File, Central Virginia Training Center, Lynchburg, Virginia.

———. (1924d). October 14 letter to H. H. Laughlin. Carrie Buck File, Central Virginia Training Center, Lynchburg, Virginia.

———. (1924e). November 1 letter to J. S. DeJarnette. Carrie Buck File, Central Virginia Training Center, Lynchburg, Virginia.

———. (1924f). November 1 letter to A. E. Strode. Carrie

Buck File, Central Virginia Training Center, Lynchburg, Virginia.

———. (1924g). December 12 letter to I. P. Whitehead. Carrie Buck File, Central Virginia Training Center, Lynchburg, Virginia.

Reed, E. W., & Reed, S. (1965). *Mental Retardation: A Family Study*. Philadelphia: W. G. Saunders.

Robertson, G. (1980). February 24 "Interest in Patient Rights Led To Sterilization Data." *Richmond Times-Dispatch*, Richmond, Virginia, pp. A-1, D-4.

Robinett, R. F. (1928). February 18 letter to J. H. Bell. Carrie Buck File, Central Virginia Training Center, Lynchburg, Virginia.

Schneider, C. (1936). (May 16 letter to H. Laughlin). *Laughlin Notebooks, Vol. II, Nazi Eugenics*. Washington University, St. Louis, Missouri.

Shockley, W. (1976). "Sterilization—A Thinking Exercise." In C. Bajema, (ed.), *Eugenics: Then and Now*. New York: Halstead Press.

Shoumatoff, A. (1985). *The Mountain of Names*. New York: Simon and Schuster.

Smith, J. D. (1985). *Minds Made Feeble*. Rockville, Maryland: Aspen Publishers.

Snyder, L. (1981). *Hitler's Third Reich: A Documentary History*. Chicago: Nelson-Hull.

Strode, A. E. (1902). December 29 letter to F. F. Voorheis. Aubrey Strode Collection, Box 81, Manuscripts Departments, University of Virginia Library, Charlottesville, Virginia.

———. (1906). February 8 letter to Dr. George T. Harris. Aubrey Strode Collection, Box 66, Manuscripts Departments, University of Virginia Library, Charlottesville, Virginia.

———. (1907). February 16 letter to L. W. Lane, Jr. Aubrey Strode Collection, Box 66, Manuscripts Departments, University of Virginia Library, Charlottesville, Virginia.

———. (1922). January 16 letter to J. C. Hudson. Aubrey Strode Collection, Box 148, Manuscripts Departments, University of Virginia Library, Charlottesville, Virginia.

———. (1924). October 7, 1924 letter to A. S. Priddy. Carrie Buck File, Central Virginia Training Center, Lynchburg, Virginia.

———. (1925). February 12 letter to J. H. Bell. Carrie Buck File, Central Virginia Training Center, Lynchburg, Virginia.

———. (1939). July 19 letter to Don Preston. Aubrey Strode Collection, Box 30, Manuscripts Departments, University of Virginia Library, Charlottesville, Virginia.

Vogt, W. (1948). *Road To Survival.* New York: William Sloane Associates.

Voorheis, F. F. (1902). December 30 letter to A. E. Strode. Aubrey Strode Collection, Box 81, Manuscripts Departments, University of Virginia Library, Charlottesville, Virginia.

Wilhelm, Caroline. (1924a). March 11 letter to A. S. Priddy. Carrie Buck File, Central Virginia Training Center, Lynchburg, Virginia.

———. (1924b). May 5 letter to A. S. Priddy. Carrie Buck File, Central Virginia Training Center, Lynchburg, Virginia.

———. (1924c). October 15 letter to A. S. Priddy. Carrie Buck File, Central Virginia Training Center, Lynchburg, Virginia.

Note

The correspondence between Harry Laughlin and Carl Schneider quoted here first appeared in a report by Randall Bird and Garland Allen in the *Journal of the History of Biology* (Fall, 1981), Vol. 14, No. 2.